The New Kindergarten:
Teaching Reading, Writing & More

BY CONSTANCE J. LEUENBERGER

SCHOLASTIC
PROFESSIONAL BOOKS

NEW YORK · TORONTO · LONDON · AUCKLAND · SYDNEY
MEXICO CITY · NEW DELHI · HONG KONG · BUENOS AIRES

Dedication

For Colbeck and Gavin, who are all my life, heart, and soul.

"We find in the beauty and happiness of children
that makes the heart too big for the body."
—Ralph Waldo Emerson

Acknowlegments

I would like to thank all of my students and their families, past and present. Without
them this book would not have been possible. I am also grateful to all of the teachers
I've met over the years who have shared ideas with me. Special thanks to my editor,
Joan Novelli, who held my hand all the way; Deborah Schecter, for her insight; and
Lauren Leon, for her artistic talent. I'd like to thank "Mama Zick" who inspired me to
fall in love with books. Big hugs and thanks to Diana, Rhonda, Joan L., Allen, Bridget,
Debbie, and Heidi for their constant support, and especially to Todd, who was Dad and
husband extraordinaire, going above and beyond the call of duty!

Produced by Joan Novelli
Cover design by James Sarfati
Interior design by LDL Designs
Cover and interior photographs by Constance J. Leuenberger and Bridget Mello,
except page 66 by Debbie Grant Photography
Interior art by James Hale

ISBN 0-439-28836-3
Copyright © 2003 by Constance J. Leuenberger
All rights reserved.
Printed in the U.S.A.
7 8 9 10   40   09 08 07

CONTENTS

ABOUT THIS BOOK

During my days I don't mingle with high-ranking CEOs, "do" power lunches with influential clients, or gaze at the view through my executive suite windows. Instead, I get to play with kindergarten children and watch their faces light up as they learn a silly new song, zip their coats by themselves, or build a block tower higher than ever. I have the opportunity to open a child's eyes to the changing seasons, to the metamorphosis of a caterpillar turning into a beautiful butterfly. I unpack peanut butter and jelly lunches and watch children climb on playground equipment, run to the finish line, and holler "Not it!" I guide their chubby hands as they learn to mix colors, bake a cake, and write their names for the first time.

Children enter kindergarten filled with wonder, hope, enthusiasm, and a love of learning. They come into the classroom eager to take on new challenges and anticipating the wonder of the "big school." They leave transformed into confident, independent thinkers and learners. Kindergarten is the most pivotal year in a child's school career. Many experts agree this is a time of profound intellectual and developmental change. By the end of kindergarten, children are thinking more logically and organizing information symbolically. They're beginning to reason and see other points of view. This is an exciting growth spurt!

My hope for you as you read this book is that you will find ideas that reflect the joy of working with kindergartners and that help you run your classroom more smoothly; that you'll be inspired to think about curriculum and instruction; and, most importantly, that you'll remember why all kindergarten teachers get up each day and head to the classroom—to teach, to cherish, and to love children.

Constance J. Levenberger

CHAPTER 1

A Day in a Kindergarten Classroom

Welcome! Our day in kindergarten begins with greetings—among students, teachers, and visitors. This community-building routine gets the day off to a warm and welcoming start, and teaches important skills, too—including listening and speaking, as well as vocabulary development. As the day goes on, children build on this predictable and positive beginning to learn literacy, math, and more. Here's a snapshot of a day in kindergarten, from greetings and morning meetings to an end-of-the-day dismissal routine that reminds students of how much they learned (and how much fun they had doing it) and makes them excited to come back again. You'll find more detailed information about each part of the day in the remaining chapters of this book.

A TYPICAL DAY

The kindergarten schedule can fluctuate depending on the time of the year. For example, in September, children may only be able to sit for a few minutes, so the morning meeting will be very brief. As time goes on and children are able to attend for longer lengths of time, the morning meeting will stretch to accommodate them.

Our Daily Schedule

8:15—8:45	Greeting/Morning Meeting/Calendar
8:45—10:30	Choice Time (Centers)
10:30—11:00	Outdoor Recess
11:00—11:30	Read Aloud and Literacy Time
11:30—12:30	Free Choice Time or Special Project
12:30—1:00	Lunch
1:00—1:20/1:40	Rest or Math
1:40—2:15	Recess
2:20—2:35	Daily News/Dismissal

BEFORE CHILDREN ARRIVE

The beginning of the school day has a lot to do with how well the rest of the day goes. When I feel prepared, and when the classroom is well stocked and ready for my students, the day runs more smoothly. Routines have a lot to do with getting off to a good start. When children arrive feeling ready for a new school day because they are familiar with the morning routines and my expectations, I know that we'll have a productive and happy day. Here are some tips for making sure you and your classroom are ready for each new day!

Make a List

When I arrive at school in the morning, I come prepared with my "To Do" list for the day. This helps to keep me focused on goals I'd like to meet by the end of the day. As I walk through the school on the way to my room, I try to cross off some of those tasks immediately. For example, if I need to drop off a report at the office, or speak with another teacher about a student, or just pick up my mail, I try to do these tasks first thing in the morning, before the children arrive.

Write a Morning Message

Once in the classroom, the first thing I do (before children get there) is write a morning message to students. I want to greet children with a literacy experience to start the day; we'll also use this letter at our daily morning meeting. This morning letter gives children a daily opportunity to understand that print conveys meaning; it also provides unlimited material for literacy activities.

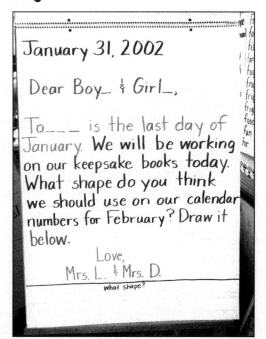

Children look forward to reading about the day's events each morning.

Especially for Half-Day Kindergarten

When scheduling children to attend either morning or afternoon programs, consult with parents to find out when their child functions best. If a child wakes up ready to go and is fading by afternoon, you will want to schedule him or her for the morning session. On the other hand, if a child has difficulty waking up and is not a "morning person," that child will benefit from attending school in the afternoon.

Check the Calendar and Choice Boards

While I'm in the morning meeting area of the classroom, I check the calendar to make sure it's ready for the day, repositioning picture cards to reflect the day's schedule. Children use "choice boards" to travel from one Choice Time activity to the next. Because students are grouped in a different Choice Time board each day, these need to be updated daily. (Detailed Choice Time plans begin on page 58.)

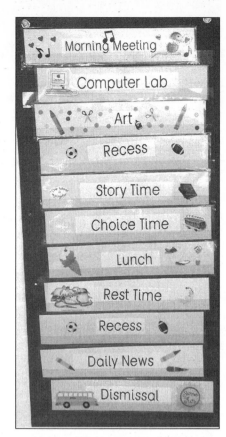

Open the Sign-In Book

Teachers have various methods for having children sign in each day. Some have a sign-in board, on which children move a tag with their name on it from the "Out" to the "In" side. I use a sign-in book, much like a guest registry for a wedding or other special event. Each day before children arrive, I make sure the book is open and ready with the correct date. (See Sign-In Book, page 10.)

Having children sign in is a good way to take attendance and to provide practice writing their names.

Set Up the Snack Table

I invite families to share a cooperative snack with the class. A sign-up sheet reminds everyone when it's their turn. If the cooperative snack is delivered before school starts, I set up the snack table. As the year goes on and children become more independent, they enjoy taking over this job. In the process, they'll make decisions about how to divide the snack equally among all students. Displaying signs that indicate the type and amount of snack provides another opportunity to meet curriculum objectives.

Children rotate to the snack table as part of their center activities.

Check Special Project Plans

I do my planning for thematic units about a month in advance, and set up whatever I need for each day's lessons the previous afternoon following dismissal. All I need to do each day, then, is a little tweaking—for example, I might plan a mini-lesson based on the previous day's events. I then check my plans for any projects I have scheduled for the day, and make sure necessary materials are ready to go. (For more on teaching with themes, see Chapter 9.) This kind of planning helps to reduce anxiety when something unexpected comes up in the morning before children arrive.

Turn legal-size copy paper horizontally to make this plan book template.

The Perfect Plan Book

I've tried several different types of plan books, none of which were ever quite right. I finally started making my own. I make a "week-at-a-glance" template on a legal-size sheet of copy paper, dividing it into five sections—one for each day of the school week. I write in all of the daily routines that don't change, such as special classes, morning meeting, rest time, and so on. I photocopy enough pages for the year and store them in a three-ring, legal-size binder. Separators for each month make it easy to refer to previous lessons if necessary.

Take One More Look

The last thing I do is make sure each center is stocked for the day. This usually takes only a few minutes, but can save precious classroom time. If all the centers are stocked, children won't interrupt me when I'm working in a small group to ask for more markers or glue.

WHEN CHILDREN ARRIVE

From "Good Morning" greetings to a community-building song, the first part of the morning is filled with opportunities for children to settle in to the new day and get started on a positive note. Here's an overview of these activities. More detailed information appears throughout the book.

Greetings

I like to greet children at the classroom door as they arrive in the morning. Their parents or caregivers are usually with them, so this gives me a moment to briefly touch base with them. Because I like to keep the morning positive, I might share a memorable anecdote about a child, or pass along some other favorable information. Children proceed by hanging up coats, unpacking backpacks, and placing any notes to me in the "Notes for the Teacher" box.

Sign-In Book

A sign-in book is a way of making each child feel a sense of belonging. To make a sign-in book, staple unlined legal-size copy paper between two large sheets of construction paper. I make a new book each month. In the beginning of the year, students use their name cards (laminated sentence strips with their names on them) to copy their names in the book. As the year progresses, children go from writing first names only to first and last (although whenever children can write both names, they're welcome to do so), and then to writing on lines. Rather than using standard lined school paper, which is spaced a bit closely for beginning writers, draw lines about two inches apart on a sheet of legal-size copy paper and then photocopy it. Some children are not yet writing their names when they come to kindergarten, and that's fine. This offers another opportunity to practice with the teacher's help.

Sign-In Assessment Tool

The sign-in book makes a great assessment tool. I save each monthly book and look back when holding parent-teacher conferences or writing report cards. The book shows each child's growth over time in handwriting skills. It's also a valuable tool for assessing children's abilities with alphabet skills, letter formation, knowledge of their name and print, and fine motor control.

Morning Message

After children sign in, they go on to read the morning message. The letter is written the same way every day until children begin to feel comfortable with it. I write each sentence in a different color marker to make it easy to differentiate one from another as students read. Many of the words in morning letters will have pictures above them to provide reading clues for children. As children read many of the same words each day, they begin to build their sight-word vocabularies. Children get a language lesson each morning without even realizing it! More detailed information on teaching with the morning message begins on page 33.

September 24

Dear Children:
Welcome to school.
Today is Monday.

Sincerely,
Mrs. Levenberger

January 7
Dear Children:
Welcome to your classroom.
Today is a beautiful day.
We will make lobsters today for our ocean unit.
What is your favorite sea creature?
Write its name below. Draw a picture.

Sincerely,
Mrs. Levenberger

A sample September letter (above) and a letter from later in the year (right).

Morning Song

When students have stopped filtering into the classroom, I put on an upbeat song in our meeting area. This signals to children that it's time to gather in the meeting area. We sing the song together, and I take time to greet any students I did not greet earlier. The morning song is another way to build literacy activities into the day. I copy morning songs onto a tagboard chart and children follow along while singing the words. Starting the day by singing together is also an excellent way to build a classroom community.

Morning Meeting and Calendar Time

Morning meeting is the time of day our class comes together as a community of learners. This is the time we practice social skills and work to create a caring community (though these both naturally carry over to the rest of the day). We take time to greet one another and discuss the day's schedule. The children also have an opportunity to share any items they may have brought from home. During Calendar Time, we reinforce math skills such as counting, even and odd numbers, and grouping. More detailed information on morning meeting begins on page 29. Plans for Calendar Time begin on page 39.

Choice Time and Centers

At the end of morning meeting, we discuss the day's agenda. When we've finished this, children get ready for Choice Time. Children rotate to various centers during Choice Time—for example, the art center, the snack center, and the math center. Step-by-step plans for setting up and teaching with centers begin on page 62.

Recess

At about 10:30 in the morning, children go out for recess and play for half an hour or so. When they return, they line up in pairs outside the classroom door and stand behind a strip of red electrical tape on the floor. The children then filter in two at a time (this helps avoid a crush when they hang up coats and get drinks at the water fountain), and then meet me in the morning meeting area for a story.

Read Aloud and Literacy Time

Children look forward to shared stories each day after morning recess. Some days I might read just one story, other days several. This is also a time to sing songs and read charts and poems. (And I make sure there's time to explore words from the stories and poems we read.) This is a favorite time of the day for all of us. Detailed plans for a literacy program begin on page 83. However, you'll find that literacy is woven into the entire day—from the morning greeting to the closing circle.

Specials and Unstructured Time

After literacy time, children either go to a special class (such as gym, art, music, library, or computers) or they have Choice Time again. As the year progresses and the first Choice Time of the day becomes more and more structured, the second Choice Time remains open. This

Especially for Half-Day Kindergarten

It's important to provide the opportunity for free exploration of centers each day, if possible. In half-day kindergartens, this time may need to be shortened to ten or fifteen minutes per day.

allows children to freely explore centers they weren't able to in the morning, and gives them the uninterrupted time they need at this age to explore their learning environment.

Time to Rest

Today with curriculum reform and standards-based testing, kindergarten teachers are feeling pressed to do more and more. But children still need time to rest. This is especially important in a full-day kindergarten. For many children who attend half-day kindergarten and then go to an after-school program for the remainder of the day, it's just as important.

In the beginning of the year, when my students return from lunch, they rest for about 30 minutes. They lie quietly on their mats while I discuss what good resting is. Like Choice Time, rest time gradually progresses into a fairly independent activity for the children. As the year goes on we begin listening to relaxing music while resting, and I eventually will place a couple of books on their mats, which children can look at during this period. If things are going well during rest time, they can quietly switch books with a neighbor.

Math Stations

As children require less time for resting, I add math into the afternoon two or three times per week, setting up math stations that children visit in pairs or small groups. Children love this math time, and ask for it often. To keep it fresh and fun, I change the stations about once a month. More information on math stations begins on page 146.

End of the Day

Just as an arrival routine helps children get ready for a happy day and a positive experience, a dismissal routine helps remind them of all the fun and learning they had and makes them excited to come back again. A brief recess just before dismissal time works well for several reasons. Many parents pick their children up from school and may arrive a little early, so recess becomes a time for parents to connect with each other and for me to connect with parents. An end-of-the-day recess is also a time-saver in winter, because students only have to get bundled up once.

Keep in Mind...

"There's nothing quite like quiet time, but few schools or classrooms have it. There's nothing like it for creating an atmosphere of calm, safety, reflection, and restoration."

—From *Time to Teach, Time to Learn: Changing the Pace of School* by Chip Wood (Northeast Foundation for Children, 1999)

When children return from recess to the classroom for dismissal, parents wait in the school lobby while we take a few minutes to discuss the day and summarize the "news" on chart paper. This is another occasion to weave in those curriculum objectives and standards. Use the daily news as an interactive writing experience, exposing children to conventions of print, such as sentence formation and standard spelling. This is also a good time to clear up any misunderstandings that children may have had with one another during the day. We then end the day as we started it, building our classroom community by singing a song.

Writing the daily news before dismissal lets children go home with the day's events fresh in their minds.

TEACHER RESOURCE

Classroom Spaces That Work by Marlynn K. Clayton with Mary Beth Forton (Northeast Foundation for Children, 2001): This book gives the nuts and bolts of setting up a classroom—great for the beginning teacher, and for all teachers looking to freshen up their programs.

CHAPTER 2

Starting The Year

"Ramona went on with her singing and skipping. 'This is a great day, a great day, a great day!' she sang, and to Ramona, who was feeling grown-up in a dress instead of play clothes, this was a great day, the greatest day of her whole life. No longer would she have to sit on her tricycle watching Beezus and Henry Huggins and the rest of the boys and girls in the neighborhood go off to school. Today she was going to school, too. Today she was going to learn to read and write and do all the things that would help her catch up with Beezus."

—from *Ramona the Pest* by Beverly Cleary (William Morrow, 1968)

Especially for Half-Day Kindergarten

Many children who attend half-day kindergarten have been attending full-day, and even five-day-per-week preschools. This is something to keep in mind while scheduling activities and sharing objectives with parents; many of the children will be able to sustain more than what might be expected at the beginning of the year.

The first day of school is so exciting! There is a sense of energy and a certain smell of new paper, paint, and a fresh classroom! Many children have been waiting for this moment for years. The agenda for the first day is to make everyone, parents and children alike, feel comfortable with this transition in life. I spend the morning greeting families and squelching fears, all the while remaining happy and positive about kindergarten. Parents may need a little extra time to separate from their children on this first day; however, five or ten minutes should suffice. Although I am compassionate about separation anxieties, I want to begin establishing a drop-off routine that will work for the whole year. Here's a closer look at the first few days and weeks of school, including how to establish the routines and expectations that will set the tone for the year, handle consequences, and begin to build a class community—one that includes children and their families.

JUST-RIGHT READ ALOUD

The Kissing Hand by Audrey Penn (Child Welfare League of America, 1993): Chester Raccoon is nervous about starting school. His mother gives him a kiss to save in the palm of his hand. This comforting story is perfect for children who are beginning kindergarten.

ESTABLISHING ROUTINES, EXPECTATIONS, AND CONSEQUENCES

The first few days and weeks of school are filled with discovery. In the midst of all the newness that is unfolding in the classroom, routines and clear expectations build a sense of security and comfort for children, and take the guesswork out of behavior. Children begin to notice the familiar pattern of the day and remember the expectations for their behavior during each part of the routine. When children know what to do and what's coming next, they feel safe in their surroundings. They're more apt to take risks as well as responsibility.

It is far easier to start off the school year with routines and expectations firmly in place than it is to make them up as you go along. Right from the start, daily routines are explicitly taught and practiced in our classroom. This begins with signing in, and continues with reading the morning message. As children move on to the morning meeting, I make sure to greet every child and try to make each one feel special. As this procedure is repeated over the first few days, children begin to form attachments and relationships with each other and with me. In the early weeks of school, some of the morning meeting time is spent on teaching expectations for using materials, behaving, and working at centers. Following are strategies for teaching expectations in these areas.

Meeting the Standards

The strong emphasis on standards in kindergarten is a reality that we all must work with. Here's an easy-to-use technique for keeping track of the many ways kindergarten activities meet the standards: Make a copy of the state and local kindergarten standards and place them in a binder. As you teach thematic units, work with children in centers, and so on, highlight all of the related standards and objectives, and record the date. This serves as a great reminder and guide, as well as evidence of having covered the standards.

Expectations for Materials

In *Guidelines for the Responsive Classroom* (The Northeast Foundation for Children, 1998), Ruth Sidney Charney, Marlynn K. Clayton, and Chip Wood suggest introducing new materials, such as markers, by hiding them in a box or bag. Children pass the bag around to each other, shaking it and calling out guesses. When the object is revealed, children can locate it in a catalog. (Be sure to have this on hand.) They're often amazed to find that a large box of markers can cost almost one hundred dollars! This kind of knowledge gives children more ownership in the materials and

Wrapping up new supplies, such as markers, makes them more special. Letting children locate materials in catalogs helps teach children the value of school supplies.

Especially for Half-Day Kindergarten

In *Beyond Discipline: From Compliance to Community* (Association for Supervision and Curriculum Development, 1996), Alfie Kohn writes, "There are so many hours in a day, and more of them should be devoted to creating a classroom where problems are unlikely to occur than to rehearsing responses to those that do occur." Troubleshoot problems to encourage independence. For example, show children how to unclog glue containers by using a paperclip to clear the opening. This is especially important in a half-day kindergarten, as time is even more limited.

makes taking care of them more meaningful. Follow these steps to make clear the expectations for using the materials and to let children practice using them appropriately:

- Discuss proper use and care of the material, then model how to use it. For example, if the item is a small bottle of glue, I show children how to open the top and spread glue on paper, and how to close the top and return the glue to the art center.

- Plan time for each child to have guided use of the material. For example, if I have just explicitly taught the use of glue in the art center, the project for the day will involve using small bottles of glue in groups of three to five students working with me at the project table. This way I can monitor behavior and encourage appropriate use of the glue.

- Let children try using the material independently. Occasionally, we'll have to revisit the proper use and care of a material if children haven't used the material in a long time, or if it is not being used properly. However, this is very rare, since so much of our time in the beginning of the year is spent on teaching the appropriate behaviors for the use and care of materials.

Expectations for Behavior

Academic learning and control of behavior go hand in hand. Learning doesn't happen when behavior is out of control. If we want to ensure children will leave kindergarten with a strong foundation of academic skills, it is important to establish expectations for behavior early in the school year. Expectations for behavior are introduced in the morning

One rule applies to most situations in a kindergarten classroom.

meeting with a discussion about caring not only for each other but also for the materials in the classroom. This leads us to the one rule in our classroom: "The Golden Rule: Treat others as you wish to be treated." I like this rule because it pertains to every situation—the way we need to treat one another, as well as belongings, classroom materials, library books, and so on. When rules and consequences become overly long and involved, children tend to mentally "check out." The Golden Rule is discussed daily for several weeks at the morning circle, and is revisited many times throughout the school day. It's fun and easy to remember, and children respond to it well. It continues to be a cornerstone for our classroom community as the year progresses.

Expectations for Choice Time

Choice Time on the first day of school is dedicated to establishing expectations for behavior and care of materials. Children are allowed to visit centers freely, trying out many or all of the centers during the Choice Time. Try these tips to help children develop appropriate Choice Time behavior:

The Math Center cubbies will be stocked with more supplies as children learn how to use them.

• Initially, stock each center with very limited materials—for example, a manipulative center might have pattern blocks. Add materials to each center over the next several weeks as children are explicitly taught how to use them.

• Keep some of the more physically active centers, such as blocks and dramatic play, closed. Add signs that read "Opening Soon for Fun-Filled Play." Allow additional time for teaching children how to take care of the materials in these centers before they are opened.

• At the end of Choice Time, clean up right beside children to model appropriate behaviors and show them where things go. After a few weeks of this, children will independently clean up the classroom.

Communicating Consequences

Along with expectations come consequences. It's essential to communicate to children from the start the consequences for inappropriate behavior. Consequences are most effective when they are related to the inappropriate behavior. For example, if children use an object inappropriately, they lose the privilege of using that object. They do not lose recess, which has no relationship to the behavior. Brief consequences, applied consistently and immediately following the inappropriate behavior, give children more opportunities to collect data and make acceptable choices. Remember that children need clean slates after breaking a rule and paying the consequence. Focus energy on encouraging positive behaviors, not dwelling on past negative behaviors.

Imagine that Clare decides to test what will happen if she paints on her neighbor's paper. A logical consequence may be that she will not be able to continue painting and must make another choice. I might say, "Clare, painting on your friend's paper is not respectful of him. You can use the paints to paint on your paper only, or you will have to make another choice." If the behavior continues, the logical response would be to calmly but immediately remove the paint boxes from Clare's work area only (but not from the other children), and tell Clare to make another choice.

Sometimes this matter-of-fact approach will cause protestations from children who want to debate the issue. When this happens, I calmly but adamantly state that I will not argue and I repeat the consequence. ("Make another choice.") Children who are inclined to test boundaries, or have watched others do so, know that I mean business, and this is usually as far as I have to go.

JUST-RIGHT READ ALOUD

Oh My Baby, Little One by Kathi Appelt (Harcourt, 2000): In rhyming text, this gentle story offers a reassuring message about the enduring love between a parent and child, as a mother bird sends her young bird off to school for the first time. You might like to share this soothing story with families, sending a copy of this book home with a different child each day.

START-THE-YEAR COMMUNITY BUILDERS

Building community begins even before the first day of school and is especially important the first few days. Following are projects, activities, and routines that are especially effective in bringing a new classroom community together—one that includes children's families.

GROUP PUZZLE: I like to start with a group project. One year I made a large puzzle out of a half sheet of plywood. I gave each child a blank puzzle piece before school started and asked them to decorate it in a way that would tell something about themselves. During the first few days of school, we put the puzzle together as we told about ourselves. This spurred a wonderful conversation about our similarities and differences. We displayed the puzzle outside our classroom for the remainder of the school year.

FAMILY QUILT: Before school starts I always have a picnic with the kindergarten families. During the picnic, I might put out fabric paint and quilt squares and ask each family to make a square about themselves. I sew the quilt together (you could also glue the squares to a flat sheet) and we hang it outside our classroom to display.

Families enjoy creating a square for our classroom quilt.

Curriculum Accountability

I'm always amazed at the amount of stress that meeting curriculum standards can cause for educators. One way to de-stress that always works for me is to simply review the state and district standards. Put check marks next to all you do in a given day or week. In the end, you will be astounded at the objectives you've met!

Have children keep a monthly growth chart graphing the size of their plant. This is a fun and easy way to build in more math skills!

GROWING WITH PLANTS: Help children develop a sense of ownership in the classroom by inviting them to bring in a small plant. These plants help create a warm, cozy feeling and give children responsibility for caring for the classroom as they water and tend to their plants. The plants also eventually can serve as a reminder of kindergarten: Many students come back to me years later and tell me that their kindergarten plant is still growing!

THESE ARE A FEW OF OUR FAVORITE THINGS: Help children and their families get to know you, and learn something about your new students, with this mini-book. Begin by making a master set of pages 25–28 in this book. To make the master, complete the first set of information on each page to tell about your own favorite things. (Add your name to the cover, too.) Photocopy a set of these pages for each child. Have children cut along the center line as indicated to separate each page. Guide children in stacking the pages in order. Staple to bind.

These Are a Few of Our Favorite Things

By ___Mrs. L.___

and ___Coby___

Have children take home the books to share with their families. They can read about your favorite things on each page, and then complete the book to tell about theirs.

FAMILY-STYLE SNACKS: An easy way to continue to build community in the classroom is to offer a cooperative, family-style snack each day. Families sign up to bring the snack one day each month. The snack is considered part of Choice Time, and is set out first thing in the morning so that children can enjoy a snack when they need it. So if children come to school hungry, they can meet that need immediately and are then free to get on with more learning. During the first few weeks of school, I spend a lot of time at the snack table. I demonstrate and model how to read and follow the snack menu, how to clean up after myself, and how to use manners. The snack table offers endless possibilities for teaching independence, responsibility, and social skills.

JUST-RIGHT READ ALOUD

The Night Before Kindergarten by Natasha Wing (Grosset & Dunlap, 2001): Told in the style of *The Night Before Christmas,* this book depicts children and their families getting ready for the first day of school. The surprise ending thrills kindergartners!

TEACHER RESOURCES

Classroom Routines That Really Work for Pre-K and Kindergarten by Kathleen Hayes and Reneé Creange (Scholastic, 2001): This guide is packed with practical tips and organizational tools for establishing and maintaining routines in the classroom.

Easy and Effective Ways to Communicate With Parents by Barbara Mariconda (Scholastic, 2003): This comprehensive guide explains how to turn every interaction with parents—from the first letter home through the last conference—into a positive, productive one. The author, a veteran teacher, provides surefire tips on how to build and maintain effective home-school communication, discuss difficult issues, and deal effectively with an upset parent.

The First Six Weeks of School by Paula Denton and Roxann Kriete (Northeast Foundation for Children, 2000): This helpful resource takes teachers through the beginning of school by week and by grade level, including kindergarten.

The First Weeks of School: Laying a Quality Foundation by Jane Perlmutter and Louise Burrell (Heinemann, 2001): Teacher reflection and common-sense advice add to this book's appeal.

Fostering Children's Social Competence: The Teacher's Role by Lilian G. Katz and Diane E. McClellan (National Association for the Education of Young Children, 1997): A great help for launching the school year, this resource includes strategies for developing children's social skills and enhancing their development.

Fresh & Fun: Back to School by Joan Novelli (Scholastic, 2002): This activity-packed book features ideas from teachers across the country. It includes community-building games, mini-books, an easy-to-learn piggyback song, poems, ready-to-use reproducibles, and a big, bright poetry poster.

Off to a Good Start: Launching the School Year (Northeast Foundation for Children, 1997): Excerpts from the Responsive Classroom Newsletter are organized into four sections: establishing rules, building a sense of group, introducing materials and the room, and extending the classroom walls (home-school connections).

Yardsticks: Children in the Classroom Ages 4–12 by Chip Wood (Northeast Foundation for Children, 1994): This is a must-have for all teachers and parents. Wood lists typical developmental characteristics for various age groups, and identifies developmentally appropriate practice in different subject areas for those age levels—always good information to review before a new school year.

These Are a Few of Our Favorite Things

By _____

and _____

Here is a picture of my family.

Draw a picture of your family here.

My favorite things to do are:

_____

_____

What are your favorite things to do?

_____

_____

3

My favorite color is: _____

What is your favorite color?

_____

Draw a picture of something that is that color.

4

The New Kindergarten: Teaching Reading, Writing & More • Scholastic Professional Books

My favorite foods are:

_____

_____

What are your favorite foods?

_____

_____

5

My favorite time of day is: _____

because: _____

_____

What is your favorite time of day?

_____

_____

6

My favorite treat is:

_____

_____

What is your favorite treat?

_____

_____ 7

- -

My favorite book is:

_____

_____

What is your favorite book?

_____

_____ 8

The New Kindergarten: Teaching Reading, Writing & More • Scholastic Professional Books

CHAPTER 3

Teaching With Morning Meeting and Morning Message

orning meeting is the most influential and important time of the day. It's the time when teacher and children come together as a community, building trust, acceptance, and support. It's a time for children to share concerns, questions, and comments about their classroom and world. Though children read the morning message as part of their morning routine, they also revisit it during the morning meeting for further literacy learning.

Morning meetings vary from classroom to classroom, taking on the flavor and tone of the particular group of people who come together. Each teacher has a different morning meeting routine. My morning meeting routines are consistent throughout the year. It's hard for us as educators to determine what may have happened to a child at home on any given morning, but we can be sure that it is comforting for them to know the school routine and the teacher's expectations.

After children arrive at school and sign their names in our sign-in book, they head over to the circle area for morning meeting. An upbeat "good morning" song signals to students that our morning meeting is about to begin. (For suggestions on great "good morning" songs, see page 32.) Children find their "circle spots" (a piece of colorful electrical tape on the floor with their name on it) and get settled on the floor. It's time for morning meeting!

BEGINNING THE MEETING

From getting children seated quietly to sharing a greeting and a song, here's how to get the morning meeting off to a good start.

Getting Settled

At the beginning of the school year, or as needed throughout the year, I use small puppets and props as "quiet tricks." I may say something such as, "This beautiful butterfly is looking for very quiet children so he can land on their shoulders." I will then touch each child gently on the shoulder with the butterfly finger puppet. I make sure every child is touched, some sooner than others. Another popular quiet trick in my class is the "magic quiet stick." This is a transparent wand, sold at many toy stores, with glitter and a thick liquid inside that flows when the stick is moved. It is very relaxing to watch as we pass it around the circle. I tell students the story of the magic quiet stick and how it has never failed to

Especially for Half-Day Kindergarten

In a half-day kindergarten, the morning meeting may need to be shortened. If need be, sprinkle literacy lessons throughout other parts of the day. Add mini-lessons during literacy time, or one-on-one during Choice Time.

make a child quiet when he or she touches it. By the time the magic quiet stick is passed back to me, the children are quiet and ready to learn. (For directions on making a magic quiet stick, see page 224.)

Sharing a Greeting

We begin each meeting with a greeting. Because many children are shy and self-conscious the first day of school, I like to keep the morning greeting simple, making children feel as comfortable as possible. Passing a smile around the circle works well. We progress into more detailed greetings as the year continues, such as the ones that follow.

SPIDER WEB GREETING: Give a child a ball of yarn. This child greets a classmate and, holding on to the end of the yarn, tosses the ball of yarn to this child. This child then greets another classmate and, holding on to a piece of the yarn, tosses the ball of yarn to that child, and so on. When the greeting is over, the circle will resemble a large spider web.

GREETINGS IN DIFFERENT LANGUAGES: Invite families or school staff who speak a language other then English to share greetings in that language. Write the greetings on sentence strips and practice them with children. Just for fun, invite everyone to use a greeting one day in any language but English.

Circle Spots

Change morning meeting assigned seats about once a month to assist with classroom management and allow children to get to know everyone in the classroom.

Taking the time to teach children how to greet others makes my expectations for friendliness and cooperation very clear from the first day of school.

Sing-Along Song Sources

Jean Feldman (also known as "Dr. Jean") is a favorite for sing-along songs. For irresistible songs that also teach early reading skills, try the following Teaching Tunes audiotape and CD sets. Each includes reproducible mini-books with song lyrics and illustrations that support the text, plus extension activities for lessons.

- Basic Concepts (audiotape; Scholastic, 2002)
- Early Phonics (audiotape; Scholastic, 2002)
- Favorite Songs (CD; Scholastic, 2002)
- Nursery Rhymes (CD; Scholastic, 2002)

PANTOMIME GREETINGS: Can children greet each other without speaking? Invite them to pantomime their greetings one morning. How many different ways can they think of?

INTERVIEW GREETINGS: Let two neighbors interview each other and share what they learned about their neighbor. This can be narrowed down to having children ask their neighbors a specific question, such as "What is your favorite time of the day and why?"

SONGS AND CHANTS: Children really enjoy these greetings. Here's a favorite, which can be accompanied by hand clapping and leg slapping:

> *We like [name].*
> *[Name] is our friend.*
> *We like [name].*
> *And here we go again!*

Morning Meeting Song Charts

During the first several weeks of school, I use the morning meeting to teach many songs that we will sing as a class throughout the year. In addition to being great community builders, the songs written on charts are powerful literacy tools. Children spend a lot of time reading these charts, and as they memorize the songs, their first reading strategies begin to develop. Old favorites, such as "Make New Friends" and "You Are My Sunshine," become favorites with students, too. Using highlighting tape and masks (see page 35 for more on masking) turns the fun of singing into valuable phonological awareness lessons!

A dowel covered with foil and topped with a sparkly star makes an appealing pointer.

TEACHING WITH THE MORNING MESSAGE

As children filter into our kindergarten classroom each morning, one of the first things they look at is the morning message that I've written to them. There is a purpose as well as motivation for reading the letter: the children want to find out about the events of the day.

In the morning message, children look for blanks that need to be filled in and sort out patterns in language.

Morning messages offer endless possibilities for building literacy skills in an authentic environment across the kindergarten curriculum. This occurs both when children read the letter as part of their morning routine and later in the day during morning message skill-building activities that may focus on phonics, introduce punctuation, or teach a math skill. For example, morning messages:

- Enhance oral language skills.
- Build phonemic and phonological awareness.
- Provide opportunities to explore written language (word families, rhyme, patterns).
- Model the features of language (sentences, words, spaces between words).
- Strengthen sight-word vocabulary.
- Develop a purpose for reading.
- Build a rich vocabulary.
- Develop handwriting skills.
- Strengthen overall confidence in literacy.

Pleasing Pointers

Decorate a coffee can and stock it with assorted pointers for teaching with the morning message. Following are some easy-to-make favorites:

- Make faces on long wooden spoons. Googly eyes are fun.
- Make a magician's wand out of a dowel. Paint it black with a white tip.
- Use glitter tubes found at toy stores.
- Use jumbo pencils bought at vacation destinations.
- Try small flashlights as fun pointers. Children can use them to highlight words as they read the room.

Building Skills

Morning message literacy skills follow a progression. In September students will be establishing one-to-one correspondence of written and spoken words. As the school year continues, they begin looking at the letters and sounds in words (graphemes and phonemes), sentence structure, and more advanced language arts skills. They explore the conventions of print, the spacing between words, the shapes and sizes of words, the left-to-right sweep of reading, and punctuation. This daily instruction is essential; research shows that explicit phonemic awareness instruction on a regular basis improves reading and spelling ability in young children.

Writing the Morning Message

Morning messages are good examples of "talk written down." Of course, many children are not conventionally reading in kindergarten, but when the language is similar each day, many begin to read the message on their own. Children also help each other read the message, and experiment with language together. Following are tips for writing effective morning messages:

- In the beginning of the year, keep the message very basic, using essentially the same language every day. As the year progresses, vary the language and leave blank spaces for children to fill in words or parts of words. (Choose letters or words that children have been working with.)
- Spell some words with dotted lines and have children trace the letters to get a sense of how it feels to write a particular word.
- Be sure to include information that children are anxious to know so that the message is meaningful for them to read.
- Use brightly colored markers and add drawings and stickers for visual appeal. Write each sentence in a different color marker to help children establish an understanding of sentences. (Scrapbooking stores are a great place to find stickers that represent everyday items.)
- Use rebus-type drawings to help the children read the letter if needed.
- To expose children to different reasons for writing, incorporate lists, schedules, recipes, and other forms of writing into your morning messages.

Morning Message Activities

After the morning greeting and song, we read the morning message as a class. In the beginning of the year I will do most of the reading and pointing to the words. As the year progresses, the helper of the day is invited to point to words as we read the message together. This allows practice in one-to-one matching of printed word to spoken word. Following are tips and activities for teaching with morning messages.

Strengthening Phonological Awareness Skills

Research indicates that children who have well-developed phonemic awareness skills learn to read more easily. It is also known that children learn best when they can make meaning from the information presented to them. Alphabet skills and phonemic awareness skills are important, but are best utilized when taught within the context of meaningful information, such as the morning message. One very useful strategy for teaching phonemic awareness is masking: asking children to find and highlight words or letters in print while blocking out the surrounding text. Use a masking technique with any of the following questions to explore relationships in language and build phonemic awareness:

- Can you find a letter in your name?
- Can you find a letter you know?
- What word begins with the same letter as your first [last] name?
- Do you see a letter that has this sound [teacher says sound]?
- Which word has [specify number] letters?
- Do you see a word that is longer than [shorter than] your name?
- Which words begin with [specify letter]?
- Which words end with [specify letter]?

Ps and Qs

Young children confuse letters that are similar in appearance, such as lowercase *p, d, b,* and *q,* and also *m, n,* and *w.* Uppercase letters such as *E* and *F, M* and *W,* and *U* and *V* are also confused. Use the morning message to reinforce recognition of these letters, letting children take turns with the pointer to find the letter *p,* for example, as many times as they can. Try not to teach letters that are easily confused together. For example, make sure children have a solid understanding of *p,* and then let some time lapse before focusing on *q.*

I Spy

Say to the children, "I spy with my little eye a word that begins with the ___ sound." Children can take turns using a pointer to identify a word in the morning message that fits. This mini-lesson usually generates conversation about letters and sounds, further reinforcing students' understanding.

Conventions of Print

Children who are exposed to print conventions are comfortable with their own early reading experiences. These questions will help:

- Where do we begin reading?
- Where do we finish reading?
- Can you show me a lowercase [uppercase] [specify letter]?
- Can you find a period [question mark, exclamation point, and so on]?
- Can you touch each word as you say it? (one-to-one correspondence)
- Can you move your hand under each word as you read along? (left-to-right sweep)

Making Masks

To make an adjustable mask children can use to highlight a single letter or an entire word, fold a 6-by-8-inch sheet of tagboard in half horizontally. Tape the bottom of the tagboard together. Cut a large, rectangular opening in both layers. Then insert a strip of tagboard into the open end. This will slide in and out to adjust the size of the opening. Here are two other easy masks to make:

- Cut brightly colored highlighting tape to the size desired. It really makes words stand out on the paper and can be used again and again. I place pieces of tape in various sizes next to the easel. Children can determine the size they will need for each task.
- Cut a "window" in several fly swatters. Children can "swat the spot" to highlight the target letter(s) or word.

- Can you show me the spaces between words?
- Show me one letter.
- Show me one word.

Swat the Spot

Children love to use a fly swatter with a rectangular hole cut from the center to play this game. A volunteer comes to the chart and holds the fly swatter. As the class sings "Round and round and round s/he goes, and where s/he stops s/he'll swat the spot!" the child turns around in front of the chart and then ends by swatting the chart. The child names whatever letter is framed by the hole in the swatter (and, later, the letter sound). Children enjoy this movement game and gain alphabet skills every time they play.

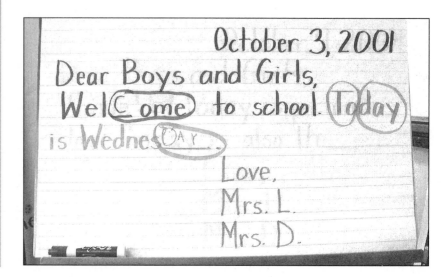

Words Within Words

Kindergartners always love this challenge. Ask them to find words hidden within words. For example, the word *today* has two words within it, *to* and *day*.

Familiar Words

Use some words on a regular basis in morning messages so that children become more familiar with them. A good strategy to use along with this is to write the word in the same color throughout the message so it stands out for children. Take a closer look at the target word in a mini-lesson. Notice features of the word, such as the number of letters, the shapes of letters, any spelling patterns, and small words within the word. Plan an activity to reinforce recognition. For example, let children use clay "snakes" to form the letters in the word.

Literacy Skill Builders

Morning meeting offers numerous junctures to interlace essential literacy skills. Listening and speaking strategies are honed during this fundamental learning time. Support children as they make contributions to the discussion, and connect their ideas to those of others. This is also a great time to build vocabulary by using word analogies and modeling descriptive words. Have fun with language using synonyms, antonyms, and homonyms! Children love playing with language, and it builds skills!

More About Words

Studying and observing different words develops vocabulary. Try having children identify different words, such as:

- Where is a word you haven't seen before?
- Can you find a word that rhymes with [specify word]?
- Can you find a word that means the same as [specify word]?
- Can you find a word that means the opposite of [specify word]?
- What do you notice about this word?
- How is [specify word] like [specify word]?

Punctuation

Later in the year, leave out punctuation at the end of sentences, and let children try to see what's missing. (Using different colored markers for each sentence helps them to find the sentences and notice the lack of punctuation more easily.) Follow up on these morning messages with mini-lessons that discuss each missing punctuation mark and have children find other examples in print around the room.

Time to Share

I send home a "sharing schedule" at the beginning of the year. Each child is scheduled to share one day per week. We adhere to that schedule all year (unless, of course, there is a share that needs prompt attention). Giving children time to think ahead about their shares encourages quality share material. Because the number of shares are limited each day, this approach also takes up less class time.

The sharing portion of the morning meeting looks very different in September than it does in June. In September, the sharing portion may simply be sharing in the traditional sense of "show and tell." Also, early on children are not expected to sit for long stretches of time, so the morning meeting—especially the sharing portion—is much shorter at the beginning of the year. Again, it's important to communicate expectations for sharing: I make it clear that I intend for everyone to feel safe and secure contributing to the group conversation. After sharing something, children ask, "Are there any questions or comments?" This routine creates opportunities to strengthen both speaking and listening skills. For example, children will be reminded to listen more closely if they ask a question that was already asked by another. With time, children become responsive, caring listeners.

In addition to children's personal shares, the morning meeting can be a time to share in other ways. For example, we might brainstorm and share

Morning Message Math Skill Builders

Morning messages are a wonderful way to integrate math lessons, too. For example, include a survey question (such as "How many pockets are on your clothes today?") and have children answer it on the message paper and sign their names. Follow up with a graphing mini-lesson that lets children work with the data they've gathered.

ideas for a new "celebration of learning" to hold at the end of a thematic unit of study. Or we might share some new playground rules and have a discussion around those. Sharing on a daily basis provides limitless opportunities for children to learn to be caring contributors to our community.

Calendar Time

Morning meeting is a great time to teach the calendar. Children are gathered in the meeting area, and it makes organizational sense to start the day reviewing calendar concepts, looking at the weather, announcing birthdays, sharing reminders about upcoming events, and so on. This also starts your day ahead of the game: A well-planned calendar session can meet all of The National Council of Teachers of Mathematics (NCTM) standards! At the beginning of the year, we might spend 10 to 20 minutes on the calendar, spending more time as the year progresses. Detailed information is outlined in the Calendar Time chapter, which begins on page 39.

Closure

We end our morning meeting by briefly discussing the plan of the day and going over center choices. I make sure children understand the objectives and expectations for Choice Time. Center setups are discussed in detail beginning on page 62.

TEACHER RESOURCES

Getting the Most Out of Morning Message and Other Shared Writing Lessons by Carleen DaCruz Payne and Mary Browning Schulman (Scholastic, 1999): This practical resource is packed with information about writing with kindergartners, including how to use literature such as nursery rhymes, songs, and poems.

Quick Tips: Morning Meeting by Joan Novelli (Scholastic, 2004): This practical guide features strategies, tips, and activities from teachers across the country for building literacy, math skills, and more with the morning meeting.

Quick Tips: Morning Message by Anne Adams, Diane Farnham, Carol McQuillen, and Donna Peabody (Scholastic, 2003): Written by four seasoned early-elementary educators, this practical resource features more than 100 ready-to-use messages that build skills in reading, writing, math, science, and more. You'll also find messages you can use to build community and celebrate special days.

CHAPTER 4

Teaching With Calendar Time

Calendar and Curriculum

Calendar Time incorporates the following curriculum objectives:

- prereading/reading skills
- alphabet skills
- exposure to literature
- color and shape concepts
- counting
- even/odd number concepts
- place value
- time concepts (clock and seasonal/monthly/daily)
- money concepts
- graphing
- spatial relations
- fine motor skills
- communication skills
- problem solving
- planning
- classifying
- sequencing
- comparing and contrasting
- creating community
- scientific process

Today Finn is very excited to be the helper of the day! He points to the days of the week as the children chant them aloud. He's gaining confidence and using math and literacy skills as he leads his classmates in a favorite morning routine: Calendar Time.

Each morning, as an extension of the morning meeting, we work on calendar activities. The calendar I use is based on the *Math Their Way* model (Center for Innovation in Education, 1990). Over the years I have added and deleted parts of the *Math Their Way* calendar so it better suits my classroom and kindergarten objectives. Teaching with the calendar gives children authentic learning experiences. A calendar is very real, and it's more exciting to count how many days until our farm field trip than it is to rote count meaningless objects. The NCTM standards tell us that children learn math concepts through everyday math activities. From checking the weather to celebrating birthdays, Calendar Time is filled with endless opportunities for them to do this.

SETTING UP A KINDERGARTEN CALENDAR

The calendar area (also known as the morning meeting area) is a dominant area of my classroom. It's where the children and I gather each morning for our meeting, and it's where we say good-bye to each other every afternoon. It's also where our read aloud and literacy activities happen. This area requires a fair amount of space, including a large bulletin board. The area also needs to accommodate the whole class sitting on the floor. For these reasons, consider doors, floor space, and traffic patterns when selecting a space.

Although setting up the calendar area might seem like an overwhelming task when you are getting started, it really is manageable if broken down into smaller parts. The best strategy is to start planning the following year's calendar at the end of the current year. That way you can enlist help from volunteers and assistants.

This chapter contains basic components of the calendar area, an overview of a sample calendar session, plus assessment and management strategies, time-saving tips, math standard correlations, home-school connections, and read-aloud recommendations.

A well-thought-out kindergarten calendar incorporates objectives across the curriculum.

Calendar Components

Calendar Grid: Cover a bulletin board with roll paper. White works well because it's appropriate for any month. Make a calendar grid on a smaller sheet of paper or tagboard (but large enough for everyone to see) and staple it to the bulletin board. Add a border to give the calendar a finished look.

Day Cards: Write the names of the days of the week on tagboard strips, decorate as desired, and laminate. On our calendar the Friday card is extra sparkly in honor of "Fantastic Friday." (See Tip at right.) Staple the cards vertically next to the calendar. Cut out an arrow and write on it "Today is." Children will move the arrow to indicate the current day.

Date Cards: Write numbers for dates (1–31) on tagboard cards (one per card) and laminate. For a surprise some months, make these cards in shapes that relate to a current theme. Try using two or three different shapes in one month (two in the beginning of the year) to build a pattern. With each new date that is added, children can guess what the next date will look like, based on the pattern they see developing. For a time-saver, check school or office supply stores for shaped note paper. You'll find it in dog, flower, rainbow, shamrock, and other shapes. Die cut machines also save time on cutting out date cards.

Fantastic Friday

Celebrate the week's learning with Fantastic Friday. Children love the anticipation of this special day, and it also serves as a good counting tool: "How many days until Fantastic Friday? Let's count." On Fantastic Friday, students have a break from the routine of the day with something fun. It might be a video related to our topic of study, a special treat during snack time, or an extended recess. It does not have to be glamorous, just something different. When planning field trips or guest speakers, I often try to schedule them for Fridays so they can be "fantastic!"

41

Especially for Half-Day Kindergarten

If the calendar session seems too long to manage first thing in the morning, use it to introduce a math lesson later in the day.

Season and Year Cards: Write the name of each season on a tagboard shape and laminate. For example, cut out an orange pumpkin for fall, a snowflake for winter, a flower for spring, and a sun for summer. Write the year on a separate card.

Month Cards: Write the names of the months on cards or sentence strips and laminate.

Days of the Week Pocket Chart: Make or purchase a pocket chart to display the days of the week. This pocket chart should have seven pockets, one for each day of the week. Use tagboard numbers (or number cards) to show the dates in the seven pockets. Display the names for the days of the week in smaller pockets under the number pockets. In smaller pockets under the numbers, display the days of the week, Sunday through Saturday. Tuck three tagboard cards reading "Yesterday," "Today," and "Tomorrow" behind the corresponding numbers. (So, if it's the 14th, the card for "Today" would appear behind the number 14, "Yesterday" is behind 13, and "Tomorrow" is behind 15.)

This calendar chart helps children understand the concept of time.

Odd and Even Chart: Choose two colors of Unifix cubes to match the current calendar color scheme and place them in containers (or set them on the chalkboard ledge, if nearby). Write "Even" and "Odd" on two tagboard cards and place them above the Unifix cubes. (Children will use these to count out each day of the month, placing them in stacks to represent the date.)

Days of School Tally: To record how many days children are in school each month, write the name of each month at the top of an

8½-by-11-inch sheet of paper (one month per sheet). Children can use a wet-erase marker to make a tally mark for each day they are in school. Along the bottom of the bulletin board, attach a strip of adding machine tape. Children will use it to record the number of days they've been in school, circling numbers that end in 0 to count by tens.

Place Value Straws: Use straws to concretely represent the days. To make place value holders for the straws, label three different-size containers "Ones," "Tens," and "Hundreds." (Ordering the containers by size—with "Ones" the smallest—gives children another visual clue for number sense and classifying objects by size.)

Weather Graph: Make a weather graph master, such as the one on page 52. (Place a couple of clean copies in your calendar supply bin, and you'll have one more piece of your calendar set up for next year ready to go.) Display a clean weather graph each month as part of the calendar setup.

Weather Graph

Name _____ Date _____

cloudy	sunny	stormy	rainy	snowy	windy

Tooth Tally: Add a tooth tally to the calendar setup to keep track of how many teeth children lose in any given month. For each month, cut out a tooth-shaped piece of white paper and frame it on construction paper. Write the name of the month at the top. Children can add a tally mark to the paper and sign their name for each tooth they lose.

Monthly Poem Pocket Chart: Display a large pocket chart for a monthly poem. I copy poems that relate to the seasons and months—line by line on sentence strips—and display a new one each month in the pocket chart.

Birthday Train: At the bottom of the calendar, I make some type of display to record children's birthdays. Some years I use premade cakes from a catalog; other years I might make a "birthday train." Whatever the display, laminate it before displaying. Use a wet-erase marker to record children's birthdays.

Calendar Bin

To save time, keep a large plastic tub near the calendar area and use it to store any supplies you might need to maintain the calendar monthly. The children will begin to know where to find the supplies, which makes it much easier for them to eventually run a calendar session and to help maintain the area. When making photocopies of weather graphs and other calendar templates, make a few extras. Paperclip them together and store them in the tub for a head start on next year's calendar!

Calendar Comparisons

Display a commercial calendar next to the class calendar so that children can make connections between the two.

Daily Schedule: Use a long, narrow pocket chart to display the daily schedule. Write each activity on a sentence strip and include a photo, if possible. Each day, arrange the sentence strips in the pocket chart vertically in the order they will occur. If the time for each activity is set, you can add this information, too. (See photo, page 8.)

A SAMPLE CALENDAR SESSION

The calendar session in my classroom builds gradually over the course of the school year. In September, when children are new to the classroom and are developmentally unable to sit for long periods of time, the calendar session lasts about five minutes. During this time, our conversations are basic, covering the date and the day of the week. We also begin keeping track of the days in school from the very first day, so that our count will be accurate throughout the year. Songs are always a welcome part of Calendar Time, especially at the beginning of the year. We sing a weather song, a days-of-the-week song, and eventually a song about the months of the year.

To meet students' developmental needs, I begin the school year explicitly teaching each aspect of the calendar. For example, we practice sitting together comfortably on the rug, listening, sharing, and gaining a sense of body space in relation to the group. Through discussion and modeling, I give students a firm understanding of the expectations I have for Calendar Time. After children become familiar with the date and day concepts, I begin to add items such as the weather graph and chart, the "Yesterday, Today, and Tomorrow" chart, and the place value exercise with straws. I usually read the monthly poem to children every morning, but only as they learn it do I expect them to join in with me. Clock activities are introduced last.

As the year progresses, children learn how to lead a calendar session on their own. My goal is to turn the calendar session over to them as soon as possible; I then act as participant and facilitator. Following is an overview of Calendar Time activities. Student helpers generally begin leading these activities about mid-year.

Classroom Helper

Because I like to keep my classroom simple, we have only one helper of the day. I string a small piece of clothesline over the calendar and attach a clothespin for each child. (The clothespins have the children's names written on them.) Each day, I pull a clothespin from the right and clip it to a small construction paper template of a person to indicate the helper of the day. When the day is over, that child's clothespin goes to the left of all the others to await another turn. The only exception to this rule is when a child has a birthday. Then the birthday child's clothespin is pulled from the line and attached to the helper figure, and that child will be the helper of the day.

Day, Month, Date, Year, Season

At the beginning of the year, I share the calendar information with children, going over the day, month, and date, and moving the arrow to the correct day card. I like to count the days with the children, so I display the date cards one at a time, with each new day.

As children become familiar with the calendar concepts, they will be able to help take them over. The helper of the day begins by asking children what the new date and day is. We read the date together as a class, with the helper pointing to the days and numbers as we read them. "Today is [month, date, year]." The helper adds the new date card in the correct pattern sequence, and moves the arrow pointing to the vertical row of days to indicate the new day. We sing a day-of-the-week song, and occasionally discuss the season and year. The helper then asks, "If today is Thursday, what was yesterday? What will tomorrow be?" The helper then places the yesterday, today, and tomorrow cards in the appropriate places in that pocket chart. (I interject to give support to the helper as often as needed.)

The helper announces the date and asks whether it is an even or odd number—for example, "Today is December 1. Is the number 1 an even or an odd number?"—then calls on a volunteer to answer. The helper places a Unifix cube on the display to indicate that the number 1 is an odd number. The following day, the helper will place a Unifix cube (in the second color) on top of this cube to indicate that 2 is an even number. Point out that even numbers are in stacks of two—they have "partners." On day 3, the helper places a cube (same color as

Comparing Calendar Data

As the year progresses, students can compare data they've gathered on the various calendar charts, graphs, and tallies. For example, they can make comparative statements about the weather, or about the number of teeth students collectively lose at different times of the year.

Stacking Unifix cubes (one each day) in two colors helps build an understanding of odd and even numbers.

45

Everyday Assessment

"Young students frequently possess greater knowledge than they are able to express in writing. Teachers need to determine what students already know and what they still have to learn. Information from a wide variety of classroom assessments—classroom routines, conversations, written work (including pictures), and observations—helps teachers plan meaningful tasks that offer support for students whose understandings are not yet complete and helps teachers challenge students who are ready to grapple with new problems and ideas." (From *Principles and Standards for School Mathematics* by the National Council of Teachers of Mathematics, 2000.) Keeping this in mind, calendar sessions serve as a great tool for young mathematicians and their assessing teacher!

for day 1) next to the stack of two cubes. Point out that this cube does not have a partner; it is an odd number. A cube gets added to this stack for day 4, giving it a partner and showing that 4 is an even number. Continue in this way through the month, stacking cubes in sets of two different colors (the same color on the bottom of each stack; the second color always on top) to reinforce the odd/even pattern.

Counting the Days

The helper moves on to add a mark to the "Number of Days in School" monthly tally. The group counts the tally marks by fives and then ones to arrive at the number of days in school for the month. A new number is added to the adding-machine-tape number line to indicate the number of days in school for the year. All numbers ending in zero are circled in a red marker; they are used to count by tens. The helper announces the number of days we've been in school for the year and adds a straw to the ones cup. If this makes 10 straws in the ones cup, those 10 straws are pulled from that cup and banded together to put as a group in the tens cup (tens are then banded to form a group of one hundred).

JUST-RIGHT READ ALOUD

The Very Hungry Caterpillar by Eric Carle (Putnam, 1983): A caterpillar eats his way through the days of the week. Invite children to retell this favorite tale in their own words, focusing on the days of the week and what the caterpillar ate on each.

Monthly Poem

We read the monthly poem together, with the helper pointing to the words. This daily repetitive reading solidifies sight-word vocabularies and introduces children to the features and functions of language. After reading the poem day after day, children begin to memorize it. This helps them feel successful with reading, and also builds a library of poems they might carry with them forever. In my classroom, I tell children that if they choose to memorize the poem (most do, but it is not required), they may recite it to me during Choice Time. When they do, I ask them to recite it for the principal as well, and they think this is great fun. They get to share their accomplishments with their larger learning community, and it's a good way to keep the principal in touch with our classroom. As you come across poems to use in your Calendar Time pocket chart, copy them on sentence strips, laminate them, and clip them together. Store them in the calendar bin to use year after year.

Weather Check

The helper calls on a weather checker to go to the window or door and check on the weather. The checker manipulates the weather song chart to indicate the correct weather and colors in the appropriate box on the weather graph. We all sing a weather song (written on a flip chart) together. We use *What's the Weather Like Today?* by Rozanne Lanczak Williams (Creative Teaching Press, 1995), which can be sung to the tune of "London Bridge Is Falling Down." I interject questions to make math con-

nections: "How many days has it been sunny this month? How many more days has it been rainy than windy? Oh, there have been four rainy days and one windy day. Hmmm… What's the difference between the two numbers? Let me think… four minus one equals three."

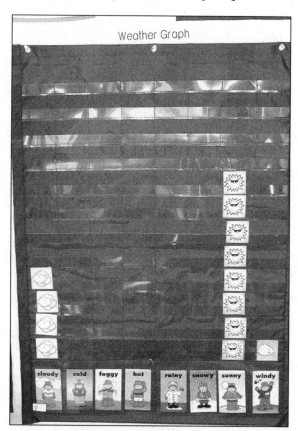

Children can make weather graphs of their own, using the template on page 52.

Tooth Tallies

Losing teeth is a big event in the early grades. Use the calendar tooth tally as needed, having children add a tally mark if they lost a tooth. At the end of each month, use the tooth tally for math discussions—for example, ask: "How many more students lost teeth this month than last?"

Daily Schedule

The helper usually sits back with the group at this point, and I take over, reviewing our daily schedule and introducing vocabulary that relates to concepts of time—for example, *before* ("What will we do before Choice Time?"), *after* ("Where do we go after Choice Time?"), and *next* ("What activity comes next?"). This review helps students to organize their day, and it is an excellent time to remind them of expected behavior. From here we break into Choice Time.

Celebrating Birthdays

Celebrate birthdays with a pocket chart song. When it's a child's birthday, display the birthday song in the poetry pocket chart. Write it in on sentence strips, cutting each line apart word by word. To save time, do this in advance for each child, and place the words in children's files. When a child is celebrating a birthday, the birthday song cards will be ready to go. Children are thrilled to walk into the classroom and see their name in the birthday song. In our classroom, this also signals that the birthday child will be the helper that day.

After singing the birthday song, we play a game with the words. To add to the effect we hum "game show" music. To play the game, mix up the word cards in each

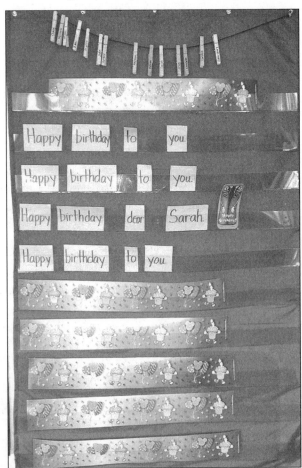

A birthday pocket chart song builds sight-word vocabulary very quickly and in a fun way!

line. Sing the song again the mixed up way. Children have to look at each word to know what they're singing, which means they're truly reading the words.

After sharing the song in a pocket chart, the child can pack up the song and take it home. Include a note inviting families to put the words in order and enjoy the song together.

JUST-RIGHT READ ALOUD

The Grouchy Ladybug by Eric Carle (HarperCollins, 1977): A grouchy ladybug picks fights with many different insects and animals (most of them much larger than she is). A clock on each page shows the time as the ladybug continues to look for a fight, making this a great book for learning time and measurement.

Calendar Clock

I use a large laminated tagboard clock with movable hands to teach time. Although I do not use this portion of the calendar in the beginning of the year, I do make sure that I have it ready before the school year starts.

MEETING THE MATH STANDARDS

A calendar session as outlined above meets expectations from all of the NCTM standards, including:

- Number and operations (counting days, place value, comparing days of different weather).
- Geometry (identifying the different shapes in which the day is written).
- Algebra (patterning the date cards, using tally marks as representations for days in school in a given month, as well as analyzing change in the number of days we have been in school).
- Measurement (comparing and contrasting the elements of time).
- Data analysis and probability (posing questions related to the passage of time, discussing events as being likely or unlikely, using graphs).
- Problem solving (counting how many days to the next holiday, or counting days to make inferences about the weather).
- Reasoning and proof (making generalizations—for example, "January is colder than September.").
- Communication (organizing mathematical knowledge as we discuss all aspects of the calendar).
- Connections (connecting the everyday use of the calendar to important math concepts, making connections between addition

and subtraction as we compare days).

- Representation (asking questions to encourage children to verbally represent their math knowledge).

KEEPING THE CALENDAR FRESH

The calendar incorporates so many areas of the curriculum, I want to be sure that students stay interested in it. Adding calendar activities gradually helps to keep it new. Monthly calendar maintenance will also help keep the calendar fresh for students. Sometimes I extend Calendar Time to include children in end-of-the-month calendar maintenance. As they become familiar with these tasks, they can take over some or all of the jobs, which include:

- Changing the border to match the new month or unit of study.
- Removing date cards. (You'll add dates to the calendar with each new day.)
- Removing the old month title and replacing it with the current month title.
- Replacing the season and year card if appropriate.
- Removing Unifix cubes. Count out 16 each of two colors, and place in the basket.
- Removing the old month tally cards (for the number of days) and replacing them with a new tally sheet.
- Removing the previous month's weather graph and replacing it with a fresh one.
- Removing the previous month's tooth tally and replacing it with a fresh one.
- Replacing the pocket chart poem with a new one.

Telling Time

To incorporate concepts of time into the day, set an alarm clock to go off every hour. Each time the alarm sounds, have children look at the clock. Guide children to state the time. You can modify the activity to focus on passage of time for five minutes, ten minutes, and so on.

TEACHER RESOURCES

Fresh & Fun: Calendar Activities by Jan Armstrong Frietag (Scholastic, 2000): This book has dozens of quick ideas to keep calendar sessions fresh and fun.

Mathematics Their Way Summary Newsletter, Cynthia Garland, principal writer and editor (Center for Innovation in Education, 1989): This is an indispensable guide for Calendar Time.

Month-by-Month Poetry: September, October & November (Scholastic, 1999), ***Month-by-Month Poetry: December, January & February*** (Scholastic, 1999), and ***Month-by-Month Poetry: March, April, May & June*** (Scholastic, 1999), all compiled by Marian Reiner: These collections feature poetry by Myra Cohn Livingston, Eve Merriam, Frank Asch, Aileen Fisher, Lilian Moore, and other favorite writers.

Teaching With the Rib-Tickling Poetry of Douglas Florian by Douglas Florian and Joan Novelli (Scholastic, November 2003): Douglas Florian is the author of many best-selling collections of poetry, including *Insectlopedia* (Harcourt, 1998) and *Bing Bang Boing* (Harcourt, 1994). This one is especially for teachers, and features dozens of new poems that connect the curriculum with the seasons.

Name _____ Date _____

Weather Graph

cloudy	sunny	stormy	rainy	snowy	windy

The New Kindergarten: Teaching Reading, Writing & More • Scholastic Professional Books

CHAPTER 5

Learning With Choice Time

One day at the dramatic play center, Elena and Carolyn decided that they needed to take a trip to the grocery store. They used the paper and pencils available at the center to make a list of all the items they needed. During their conversation about the list, they collaborated about the spelling of words, and stretched the sounds of words as they spelled them phonetically.

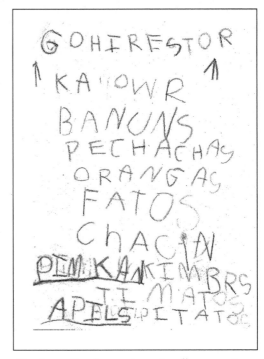

The dramatic play center naturally connects literacy skills, here in a grocery list.

Elena and Carolyn were playing—but at the same time, they were exploring language and building literacy skills on many levels. These girls needed to make a shopping list so that they would know what to buy at the store. The list served a function—a reason for them to write. While writing the list, they experimented with different features of language, such as phonetic sounds and grammar. For example, although the spelling of the list is not conventional, they showed their knowledge of language and how print works. They wrote the items in list form, showing their knowledge of how lists are made. The words are written in a linear fashion, from left to right, showing their familiarity with print. They worked together to listen to the sounds of each word they wrote, and came pretty close with many of the words. The list shows that they know many letter sounds and understand how to break the words into syllables. Working together, they learned from each other, scaffolding information to new levels.

A carefully planned and structured learning environment, such as the dramatic play center Elena and Carolyn worked at, nurtures essential skills in many ways. The center is equipped with books, writing tools, and related materials, all of which invite children to explore literacy as they participate in center activities. This chapter offers a framework for teaching with Choice Time that includes:

• Suggestions for classroom setup (page 55).

Time for Exploration

Research shows that young children learn best through experimentation, play, and opportunities to explore and discover their world. In the process, they make meaningful connections between their ideas and knowledge. Choice Time in the classroom provides such an environment, one that invites children to explore centers at their own pace and construct knowledge from their experiences.

- Tips for maintaining centers (page 57).
- A step-by-step plan for introducing students to centers and easing the way for independence (page 58).
- Strategies for center management and assessment (page 60).
- Detailed plans for four centers—blocks, dramatic play, reading, and writing—and starter plans for art, math, and science centers (pages 62–81).

DESIGNING CENTER SPACES

A center is a self-contained area of the classroom dedicated to exploration of a particular subject or material—such as blocks at the block center, manipulatives at a math center, and books on tape at the reading center. The first step in using centers during Choice Time is to plan the physical environment, keeping your goals for the classroom in mind. For example, is it important to you that each child feel that he or she can be a part of the group, but also have opportunities for alone time as needed? Along with group areas, you might want to consider cozy, quiet, alone spaces as well. Is your goal for children to become independent and self-sufficient in taking care of their needs? You might want to consider putting the snack and art centers near the sink area so children can easily clean up after themselves. In keeping with a child-centered philosophy, the physical space must be created at children's eye level, with supplies and materials they can easily reach (including those needed for cleanup).

In considering the physical space for centers, practicalities must also be kept in mind. Centers that require quiet and concentration need to be placed away from centers that are more active and loud. Unique areas in your classroom should also be considered. For example, in a previous classroom, I had an alcove with built-in bookshelves that was ideal for my reading center. Other considerations include:

- Which centers would work best in corners?
- Which centers might require electrical outlets?
- Which centers need to be located close to the sink or on flooring that is easily cleaned?
- Would you like children to have a window in the science center to observe the outdoors and have sunlight for growing things?
- Which centers need lots of floor space, or require areas for tables and chairs?

Especially for Half-Day Kindergarten

Children need to have time each day to choose what they will learn and to explore their learning environment. To manage Choice Time in a half-day program, try running activities simultaneously, facilitating small groups working on the required curriculum work while the other children engage in Choice Time. Try to schedule most of the required curriculum work into centers and small-group work. If this seems like too much, try running Choice Time every other day.

Designing a Floor Plan

I use grid paper to make a floor plan, remembering to include doorways, windows, bathrooms, and any other permanent features of the classroom. I like to make one floor plan that incorporates furnishings that I wish I had and one floor plan that is realistic, based on the furnishings I do have. This system helps me to think creatively, instead of feeling limited by budgets and furniture. It also encourages me to find desired items at yard sales, in the school basement, or in my own attic!

With these questions in mind, consider overall visibility: children need to be visible to the teacher from all areas of the classroom, as well as the teacher to children. In *Teaching Children to Care: Management in the Responsive Classroom* (Northeast Foundation for Children, 1992), Ruth Sidney Charney explains: "…children need to be seen. [It's] a simple matter of safety and a more complex matter of recognition and trust. Developmental studies tell us that six-year-olds need to be seen so they will not climb walls. Fives need to be seen so that they can be free to venture off, leave the enclosure of the teacher for experiences with play and work."

As you plan center locations, keep the following in mind:

• Setting up centers around the outside of the classroom leaves a natural open area for morning meeting and group activities. Depending on the group of children and the types of centers you have, this can either be a help or a hindrance; too much open space encourages running and off-task behavior in some students.

• To help children work within a particular center, create natural boundaries with furniture. Strips of colorful electrical tape on the floor can also indicate boundaries.

• When setting up the classroom environment, try to balance soft and hard surfaces. Children need hard surfaces upon which to write and work, but they also need the soft surfaces provided by rugs and pillows where they can relax while reading or listening to a book, or go to be alone and think independently.

Position bookshelves to help create corners in the classroom for centers.

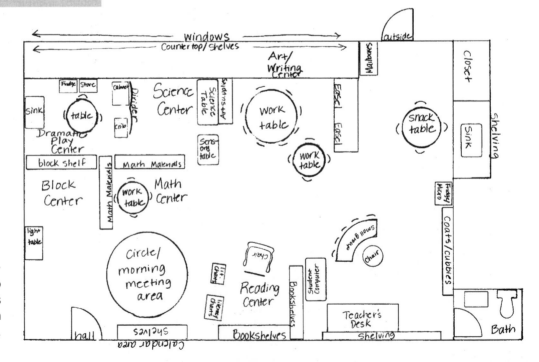

MAINTAINING CENTERS

Maintaining centers that are interesting, neat, and attractive begins by explicitly teaching children how to use and care for them. At the beginning of the school year, materials should be kept to a minimum and added to daily as children are taught—through discussion, modeling, and role playing—how to maintain each center. Large centers with many materials are not opened until you have had an opportunity to teach children how to use them. Other tips for maintaining centers include the following:

- To encourage independence, organize materials so that they are easy to find and take care of. Using both words and pictures, label tubs or other receptacles for storing materials at each center. Store them on low, open shelves that are easily accessed by children.

- Trace an outline of materials on contact paper. Cut out and adhere the outlines to shelves so children know exactly where to return items. (This works well for staplers, tape, and writing utensils). This is also a good way for students to use their matching skills! Storing items that are used daily in the same place all year saves time by helping children to know exactly where to return them.

- Adequately stock centers. This saves classroom time.

- Keep centers clean and organized. This makes it easier for all classroom members to find things, and makes the centers inviting for children. Some children cannot think in disarray.

- A bleach and water solution (1/4 teaspoon bleach to 1 quart warm water) works well for wiping down surfaces at centers and cleaning materials that come in close contact with many children, such as manipulatives at the math center and toy foods at the dramatic play center. This helps cut back on the spread of germs. (This solution is, of course, for teacher use only. Label the solution and list its contents, and keep out of children's reach.)

- Be creative with centers and update them frequently. This helps keep interest high and children on task. Sometimes just a few minor changes help to spark new interest. Rotating materials— for example, reintroducing a game or science tool in February that students last used in September—can be just as successful as introducing new items.

Small Spaces

If your space is quite small, you might consider using traveling centers: Place center activities in baskets that children can take to available areas of the classroom. Another factor to consider is furniture: If you have too much, you might want to get rid of some of it to give children more room in which to work and move around in. Organize supplies and materials neatly in tubs and baskets to make the most of center space.

Tip

Grand Opening

In the beginning of the school year, when some centers remain closed until children have learned how to properly use and care for the materials, I string a crepe paper ribbon across the center and hang a sign that reads "Opening Soon!" When children are ready to use the center, we have a ribbon cutting ceremony to open it.

ORGANIZING CHOICE TIME

Children begin using the centers on the first day of school; however their time at the centers looks very different a few months into the school year. Here's a four-phase plan for introducing centers and making them work.

Step One: Free Choice

On the first day of school, Choice Time is "free choice" time. Children are free to explore the centers of the room during the entire Choice Time block. Some of the larger, higher-maintenance centers—such as blocks and dramatic play—are closed at the beginning of the year so that children can first learn how to work at centers with limited, familiar materials. For example, the art center will be open but the easel portion of it will be closed. (For more on introducing new materials, see page 17.) This free choice phase of Choice Time is continued until I begin to notice that children need more direction and structure.

Step Two: Center Cards

During the second phase of Choice Time (which begins in the second or third week of school), I display cards with a center name written on each. I make as many cards for each center as the maximum number of students I want working at the center. So if the limit at the block center is four students, there are four block center cards. Each center card includes a photo or image to indicate the center. Kindergartners love glitter, so decorative cards are extra appealing.

At the conclusion of the morning meeting, we play a game that helps to organize students for Choice Time. To play, hold up the center cards, with the cards facing away from children, and let each child choose a card. Make a big deal about the

Center cards clearly indicate the activity. There are as many cards for each center as students who can work there.

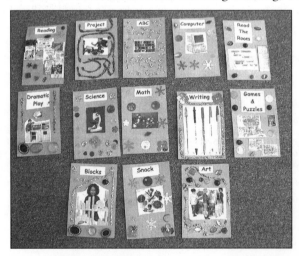

58

centers they choose. ("Oh, Cole! You're so lucky; you have a chance to visit the reading center today!") Even if this child was hoping to go to the block center, the excitement will be catching and the reading center will become a terrific destination. Whereas at the beginning of the year, children moved from center to center as they wished, this phase gets them used to staying at one center for a sustained period of time, and also gets them to try centers they might not have chosen on their own. Children stay at their assigned centers for about 10 to 15 minutes, and then make other choices and move freely throughout the room.

Step Three: Choice Boards

The next phase of choice time involves a choice board. This phase starts somewhere between the fourth and eighth week of school, depending on the group of children and how they are working together. Choice boards are a Choice Time management system that works well for my classroom. Choice boards direct a group of children from one group of centers to another over a period of one week. The choice board assignments change each week to regroup children and change the center rotation. For example, if there are four different color choice boards in the order (from left to right) of red, orange, yellow, green, then a child's rotation might look like this: On Monday, if the child is on the first (red) choice board, he or she will then move to the orange choice board on Tuesday, the yellow on Wednesday, and so on. This is also a great tool for the children to practice left to right sweep, as in reading. There are endless other management systems that also work, such as center necklaces with punch cards, hooks and tags, clothespin charts, weekly graphs, and student plans. It's important to choose a system that works best for your students and your classroom.

To make choice boards for a group of approximately 16 to 24 children, follow these steps:

- Select four large sheets of construction paper, each a different color. (There will be a red choice board, a yellow choice board, and so on.)
- Create symbols to represent each center (or use photographs). Glue

Home-School Connection

At open house or curriculum night, post lists of what children are learning while they work in each center. This will help to expand parents' view of play and its value in the classroom. (Each detailed center writeup presented here includes a list of skills and concepts that you can use as a resource.)

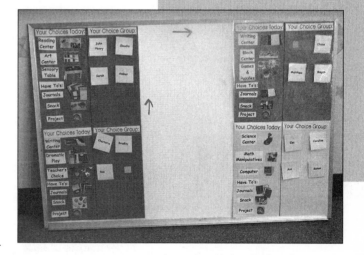

Choice boards let children know which centers they can choose from each week.

59

Line Up!

Choice board groupings are convenient to use if children need to line up quickly to go somewhere. For example, if the school nurse is doing vision and hearing checks, you can call children by choice board groups to leave the room together. This is sometimes more manageable than having the entire class line up, and it lets most of the group continue working until it's time for the next group to go.

various combinations of the center symbols on the four different choice boards, up to six works well—for example, one choice board might picture the following centers: art, reading, blocks, math, writing, and science. Try to include some quiet centers as well as more active centers on each board. Choice boards can overlap—for example, the reading center might be on the red choice board and on the purple choice board.

• Laminate the choice boards so that they will last the remainder of the school year, and then attach as many pieces of Velcro to the outside edge as there will be students in a group. (Five is usually about right.)

• Write each child's name on a small tagboard card. Laminate the cards and attach Velcro to the back of each.

• Arrange the name cards on the choice boards to form center groups. The children assigned to each choice board will choose their centers from that board. Note that choice boards just let children know which centers they can choose from. They do not need to rotate with the other children on that board to each center. In this way, children remain an active part of the decision-making process for their learning.

MANAGEMENT STRATEGIES

Choice Time might involve weeks of prior planning, a beautiful classroom set up, fabulous learning materials, and a small class size, but it will not succeed if there is no classroom management. Here are some tips for managing your classroom effectively:

SET EXPECTATIONS: Explicitly teach children how to use and care for all materials. Discuss and model appropriate behaviors and use role-playing situations to illustrate appropriate use of materials. Make expectations clear and enforce consequences when expectations aren't met. Clear and concise management strategies are the first step in a solid academic kindergarten program, giving the children the start they'll need to develop their skills. (For more on classroom management techniques, see pages 17–20.)

HANDLE DISRUPTIONS: When disruptive behavior or conflicts erupt during Choice Time, remind the students involved of the expectations. If needed, remove them from the group, and give them time to think of better ways to handle the situation. Before they return to the group, discuss the issue with them. Keep these discussions brief and firm.

RECOGNIZE WHEN IT'S NOT WORKING: Any time that Choice Time seems to be spiraling out of control, I stop children for a class meeting about what wasn't working, and we brainstorm ways to fix it. In the beginning of the school year, you may have to use this tactic quite often. However, if used consistently and productively early on, problems will be nearly nonexistent by the middle of the school year or before.

ASSESSMENT STRATEGIES

Here's a system for writing anecdotal records that I have found helpful. At the beginning of each year, divide the inside of one or two manila file folders (depending on the num-

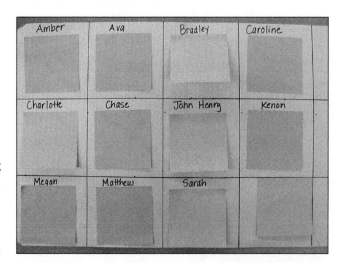

Sticky notes on the inside of a file folder are a handy way to organize anecdotal records.

ber of children) into small squares, just large enough to hold a standard-sized sticky note. Write each child's name in a square. As you observe children at Choice Time, write anecdotal records on the sticky notes and put them under the corresponding child's name. Later, remove the sticky notes and place them in a binder in which you've placed and labeled several sheets of paper for each child. These notes come in handy when it's time to write reports and hold conferences.

Pocket Jobs

When children are moving through the routine of Choice Time easily—using their choice boards, making decisions about their learning, and demonstrating on-task behavior—I begin to add "pocket jobs" each week. These are specific jobs that relate to a current unit of study. I ask children to complete one job per day, Monday through Thursday.

Instructions for pocket jobs are displayed in clear Plexiglass "pocket" frames and are set up at centers that most closely match the activity of the pocket job.

SAMPLE CENTER SETUPS

When choosing centers to include for Choice Time, start small, planning a few centers that support both curriculum objectives and the goals you have for your students and yourself. You might consider an art center, a dramatic play center, and a reading center. As the school year progresses, you can add new centers and integrate new materials into current centers. Following are detailed plans for four centers—blocks, dramatic play, reading, and writing—as well as starter plans for art, math, and science centers (pages 76–81).

Block Center

Children learn concepts of gravity, balance, and stability as they build with blocks.

There is a building boom in the block center today. Paul and Eliza have built an elaborate zoo with cages and corrals for the many plastic animals. There is even a tank (made from a borrowed fish bowl) that houses marine animals. It's almost time for recess, and they would like to keep their structure standing for a while longer, so they are in the process of writing a note, asking the class to please save it. They've used collaboration and cooperation today in the block area, implementing many other skills ranging from measurement to literacy.

Not only is playing with blocks a wonderful open-ended activity that stimulates the imagination, it encompasses every curriculum objective imaginable! Children make up stories as they build with blocks; use classification and planning skills; and experiment with pattern, balance, shape, and design. They work small muscles and cooperate with one another as they build whole cities and environments. I often have older students come back to my classroom and ask to build with blocks. Block building is meaningful learning at its best.

Block Center Setup

The block center should include an area of floor space for building—the bigger the better. Block building usually requires a lot of talking and working together, so locate this center away from others that require intense concentration. Here are a few other considerations to keep in mind:

• Because of large structures created in the block center, boundaries must be well marked. Our floor is marked with colorful electrical-tape boundaries so children know how far out they can build without interrupting the play of others working in different centers.

• Block building is very active, both physically and mentally; for this reason, the number of children allowed at the center at one time should be kept to a minimum. Smaller groups of children (two is the limit in our classroom) allow for more room for building and movement at the center, and less risk of off-task behaviors.

• The big wooden blocks that are the backbone of the block center are stored on wooden shelves in my classroom. Contact paper in the shape of blocks is adhered to the shelves to let children know where to stack the blocks when they are finished using them.

• Small bins labeled with words and pictures make it easy for children to put away props. To keep the block center fresh all year, be sure to rotate materials and toys, including items that are currently being studied or that are of great interest to the children.

Supply List

Consider the following materials for a well-stocked block center:

✓ various blocks (For block-making ideas, see page 224.)
✓ train set
✓ marbles
✓ cardboard tubes
✓ measuring tools
✓ small boxes
✓ small pieces of fabric for making tents and enclosures
✓ aluminum foil for making windows and shiny buildings
✓ dollhouses and accessories
✓ puppets
✓ small street signs
✓ carpenter aprons
✓ hardhats
✓ tools
✓ sample blueprints
✓ large white paper to make blueprints
✓ blue crayons/markers to make blueprints
✓ play carpenter's angle and drafting tools
✓ pictures of construction
✓ pictures of various buildings
✓ plastic animals (farm, jungle, sea, pets)
✓ toy vehicles and people
✓ a rug with roads/cities on it

JUST-RIGHT READ ALOUD

Changes, Changes by Pat Hutchins (Macmillan, 1987): This wordless book depicts two toy people building and rebuilding a structure, perfect for inspiring children's own block-building adventures.

Carpenter Aprons

Inexpensive fabric carpenter aprons can be purchased at home supply stores. These aprons have two pockets in the front for young builders to store their tools.

Skills and Concepts

The blocks in my classroom are a big attraction at the beginning of the school year. Children spend much of their time exploring blocks and laying them end to end to make long trains, or building tall towers and knocking them over, experimenting with the scientific concepts of gravity, balance, and stability. Through this free exploration, they begin to understand weight, texture, shape, and size. As their experiences with blocks broaden, they begin to travel through specific developmental stages in their play with blocks. These stages are, like the blocks themselves, built one on top of the other. A child will master one stage of block building before going on to the next.

After building many trains and towers, children begin to learn the concept of bridging. This involves standing two blocks on end vertically with a space between them, and laying another block across horizontally. Once again, much practice and problem solving is involved in the process of building bridges.

The next stage in block building is making enclosures. This is where children put several blocks together to build structures that are enclosed in some way. Soon after enclosures are made, the representational stage of block building begins. Buildings become places such as zoos, houses, farms, and aquariums. Children use language, creativity, cooperation, and imagination to build and name these enclosures. This is a wonderful stage to incorporate plastic animals and small people—the zoos and houses all need inhabitants!

When children build a particularly large structure, I forewarn them of clean up a little earlier than the rest of the class. This gives them extra time to put away all of the blocks, or to make a sign indicating that they would like their structure saved for a while.

After children have had a great deal of free exploration with the blocks, and have progressed through most of the developmental stages of block building, I begin to raise the expectations. We review The Golden Rule (see page 19) and apply it to the care of blocks. Children are now expected to take structures apart, instead of knocking them over. We continue to fine-tune social skills at the block center and extend the care of materials. Other important concepts children learn include, but are not limited to, the following:

- spatial relations
- measurement
- counting
- size, including depth, width, height, and length
- symmetry
- balance
- classifying and sorting
- patterns
- hypothesizing

- weight
- gravity
- cause and effect
- force
- fine and gross motor skills
- organization
- creativity
- problem solving
- language skills
- care of materials

JUST-RIGHT READ ALOUD

Building a House
by Byron Barton (Greenwillow Books, 1990): Bold illustrations and simple, step-by-step text show how a house is built, making this a great book for the block center.

CENTER TALK: BLOCKS

Tom and Taymon are building a zoo out of blocks. In this brief conversation, the teacher guides them in using problem-solving skills.

TAYMON: The alligators need to go over here. *(Pointing to a distance away from the zoo).*

TOM: That's too far.

TAYMON: No.

TEACHER: Why do you want the alligators over there *(pointing),* Taymon?

TAYMON: To keep them away from the other animals.

TEACHER: Will the alligators be able to get out? How do you think you could build their cage so they won't get out?

TOM: We can build it high.

TEACHER: Is there another kind of cage that would be used for an alligator?

TAYMON: I saw them in a glass cage once.

TEACHER: Do you think that would hold them inside?

Dramatic Play Center

Recently a student in our class broke his arm. This led to a discussion about casts and going to the hospital. The discussion prompted a field trip to the local hospital, which then led to setting up our own hospital in the dramatic play area of the classroom. Children brought in doctor kits of all kinds. Two classroom parents who are physicians offered additional props and materials for our hospital.

Children make sense of their world at the dramatic play center through active involvement and social interactions with others. They develop necessary literacy skills as they plan, connect concepts, discuss ideas, and record reactions and observations. The play here is rich and noncompetitive, and the learning occurs naturally.

Dramatic Play Center Setup

The dramatic play area in my classroom is set up in a corner with a window, adjacent to the block center—both active, language-filled centers. Corners or other areas that are partitioned off in some fashion work well in creating a cozy atmosphere for dramatic play environments. Other setup considerations include:

• The area should be fairly large, allowing enough room for small furniture and materials needed to create dramatic play environments.

- The play at this center is open-ended and very social, incorporating many language skills. For this reason, it is best to establish a dramatic play center away from quiet centers.
- In September, when school begins, set up the dramatic play area for "housekeeping." Children enjoy the free play with realistic props and materials.
- As the school year continues, vary the dramatic play center (about once a month) to reflect thematic units and children's interests. (For variations on the dramatic play center, see the Tip on page 68.)

Supply List

(for a basic "housekeeping" dramatic play center)

- ✓ empty food containers (plastic bottles, boxes)
- ✓ telephone book
- ✓ blank recipes
- ✓ dolls
- ✓ dress up clothes (consider all cultures)
- ✓ telephones (pretend or real, with the cords cut off)
- ✓ grooming utensils (blow dryers, curling irons, etc., with the cords cut off)
- ✓ small kitchen appliances (mixers, toasters, etc., with the cords cut off)
- ✓ play sink, stove, refrigerator
- ✓ home furnishings
- ✓ assorted clothes
- ✓ utensils
- ✓ pots, pans, dishes
- ✓ place mats

- ✓ clothespins and line
- ✓ towels
- ✓ pretend food (consider all cultures)
- ✓ small broom, vacuum
- ✓ aprons
- ✓ old camera
- ✓ coupons, grocery store flyers
- ✓ recipe cards, cookbooks, cooking magazines
- ✓ play money
- ✓ check book registers, pretend checks
- ✓ calendars
- ✓ message board
- ✓ mirror
- ✓ rugs
- ✓ plants
- ✓ pillows
- ✓ knick knacks
- ✓ old computer

Cultural Connections

When creating dramatic play environments, it's important to represent various cultures, including those represented in the classroom. Be sure to include some ethnic food or products specifically used by various ethnic groups. This is a good time to discuss cultural differences among the children, celebrating each family's unique traditions and customs.

Skills and Concepts

Most kindergarten children come to school ready to play. They head to the dramatic play area and begin playing with classmates, exploring the environment and using actions to express their thoughts. They engage in conversations with others as needed to share ideas and materials, learning

More Dramatic Play Centers

Children's natural curiosity about their world, coupled with thematic units of study, provide a plethora of possibilities for centers. In addition to the ideas developed in this section, you might consider the following:

- garden center
- restaurant
- bakery
- bank
- office
- circus
- veterinarian's office
- gas station
- any type of store (grocery, department, pet, shoe, craft)
- school
- travel agency
- doctor's office/hospital
- post office
- fire house

through language and social interaction. Children are gaining critical literacy and academic skills as they work together in the dramatic play area, they just don't realize it because they are so busy having fun! Important skills and concepts children learn include, but are not limited to, the following:

- making choices
- cooperating
- expressing feelings
- communicating
- problem solving
- planning
- learning about adult/family roles
- sharing and compromising
- using imagination
- connecting ideas and experiences
- enriching vocabulary
- rehearsing ideas
- organizing information
- representing knowledge

Because children are at various developmental levels, we must take into consideration the whole spectrum of behaviors displayed at the dramatic play center at any given time in the school year. Here's an overview of what you might see, based on students' developmental levels:

PRE-INTERACTIVE: When children are first exposed to a new environment, such as dramatic play, they spend a good deal of time sizing up the situation. They say very little, but are assimilating all the information they see and hear. This is an important stage in the development of play; it allows children to acclimate themselves to the situation. Children at this stage may ask questions, or offer comments, but the play is not yet interactive.

PARALLEL PLAY: In the parallel play stage, children wander less, but play alone. They may play with materials and props in the dramatic play area, but will have no interest in playing with other children. This time is for discovery on their own. Eventually children will begin to play next to other children, but not necessarily with them. They may play with the same props and materials, but will not interact with each other; the play is very much singular.

INTERACTIVE PLAY: The interactive play stage is where many children are upon entering kindergarten. They will play with other children at the dramatic play area; however, they do not discuss or plan the course their play will take. This stage of development generally lasts

68

quite awhile, and requires many opportunities to discover, imagine, experiment, problem solve, and wonder. At this time, providing materials that rein in open-ended exploration can meet academic objectives and still be developmentally appropriate. For example, a message pad and pencil invite children to write out a pretend phone message far better than a stack of blank papers and a box of crayons.

PLAYING WITH PURPOSE: In the final stage of play, children are busy creating roles to use in intricate skits and role-playing environments. Children work together, discussing and fine tuning the "rules" of play. They negotiate turn-taking and the use of materials with each other. They are playing with a purpose, using their intrinsic motivation to construct knowledge about their world.

CENTER TALK: DRAMATIC PLAY

Charlotte and Leandro are serving the teacher in the Kindergarten Restaurant. The teacher orders a hotdog, and guides the children in using what they know about letters and sounds to spell the word.

CHARLOTTE: We need to write down *hotdog* on the paper.

LEANDRO: How do you spell *hotdog*?

CHARLOTTE: *(Begins to sound out the letters and write the letters to correspond with each sound.)*

LEANDRO: *(To the teacher)* Does this spell *hotdog*?

TEACHER: Do you think this spells *hotdog*?

LEANDRO: Yes.

TEACHER: Let's look at the letters together. Can you give me the sounds of the letters as we read it together?

LEANDRO, CHARLOTTE, TEACHER: *(Sounding out the letters)* H-T-D

TEACHER: Do you know how to spell *dog*?

LEANDRO: D-O-G

TEACHER: *Dog* is part of *hotdog*. Where do you think it might go?

CHARLOTTE: I know! At the end! H-T-D-O-G!

Home-School Connection

Play often looks different at school than it does at home. Help parents see that when children play at home it is usually free play with little structure. At school, the play is very structured, teacher facilitated, and loaded with learning. Pointing out the differences between the two play atmospheres will help parents understand the learning that takes place in the classroom. But remember, both kinds of play are important!

Reading Center

Today at the reading center, Rhonda and Renee are reading song charts. As they sing and point with special wands, they are learning the left-to-right progression of words and the return sweep, as well as the one-to-one correspondence of written word to spoken word. Meanwhile, Sam listens to a story on tape that he and his mom have recorded for the class; it's comforting to hear his mom's voice as he listens to a favorite story. Paul sits in the large, comfy rocker with a stack of books on his lap, flipping through each one, looking at the pictures, and telling a story.

A comfortable chair is an inviting addition to a reading center.

All of these children are using prereading and reading strategies as they go about their various activities. They know that print carries a message, and are beginning to understand how print is organized. They recognize the significance of spaces between words, as well as the differences between letters and words. They are using their phonics skills to decode unknown words and can relate the themes found in these stories and songs. A reading center incorporates learning on many levels, and supports the many ways children learn best.

Reading Center Setup

The reading center works best in a cozy corner of the room where children feel comfortable and can relax with a good book. Other considerations include the following:

Set up the reading center away from centers that tend to be noisy, such as the dramatic play and block centers.

• When choosing books for a reading center, be sure to include multilingual books, as well as books that represent various genres. Song books are fun for children, as are Big Books, mini-books, and books on CD. Store books in baskets grouped by author or subject.

• Make place holders for children to mark the basket or place on the shelf from which they took a book: Cut strips of tagboard and write each child's name on a couple of them. Laminate these for use all year; they will help children to reshelve their books more quickly as they get ready to finish up at the center.

- When labeling the classroom with literacy labels, make two sets for each item. Put one label on the item; put the other label in the reading center. Children can use these to match the two labels while "reading the room." This is a concrete way for children to immerse themselves in environmental print, comparing and contrasting the shapes and features of words.

- Make a reading corner more inviting by adding a small sofa, end table, and lamp. A wading pool filled with comfy rugs and pillows is lots of fun, too!

Supply List

In addition to a variety of books (song books, picture dictionaries, alphabet and wordless books, class-made and student-published books, easy readers, and so on), consider the following materials for a reading center:

✓ literacy and song charts

✓ pointers (see page 33)

✓ comfortable chairs

✓ picture dictionaries

✓ magazines and catalogs

✓ maps

✓ newspaper "funny pages"

✓ books on tape

✓ tape recorder

✓ headphones

✓ a class list on a chart

✓ copies of old morning messages

✓ letters from pen pals

✓ menus

✓ bookmarks

✓ flannel board with characters for story retellings

✓ magnetic boards

✓ magnetic props and letters

✓ author posters

Skills and Concepts

The reading center is a natural environment for building essential literacy skills, including:

- phonemic awareness

- alphabet skills

- experiencing the features and functions of language and how language relates to print

- listening and speaking skills

- conventions of print

- understanding that print conveys meaning

- phonological skills

TiP

Spaceship Reading Corner

Paint a refrigerator box to make a spaceship. Punch holes in the top and string with twinkle lights. Plug in the lights and let children read inside wearing headphones (to listen to mission control—and to create a quiet atmosphere for reading).

TiP

Books on Tape

Enlist volunteers (such as parents and senior citizens) to record books on tape. Provide each volunteer with the book, blank tape, and small bell (to ring when it's time to turn the page). Parents can record the book as they read it to their child.

- structural analysis (prefixes, suffixes, root words, compound words)
- vocabulary and sight word development
- self-correction strategies
- comprehension skills
- storytelling
- care of books
- exposure to different genres
- imagination
- fine motor skills

Many kindergarten children do not have the physical capabilities needed to sweep their eyes from left to right across a printed page. They tend to focus on one item at a time, and therefore formal reading instruction should not be an expectation for kindergarten children. Of course, literacy activities should always be encouraged, with the understanding that all children should not be expected to read independently in kindergarten. As children are immersed in literature and are given meaningful experiences and a chance to practice newly acquired skills, they will become readers. With this in mind, learning at the reading center usually progresses in the following stages:

- In the beginning of the school year, children browse the books and become familiar with them. This is a good time to have plenty of books on tape for children to listen to as they follow along.

- As the year progresses and children have heard and read many books during story and literacy time, they'll begin to use pointers and reread the books and charts they are familiar with. This is a wonderful and meaningful way to build sight-word vocabulary.

- As children write their own books, add these to the classroom library and reading center. This provides predictable books that children can read on their own by the end of the year, and it celebrates their work as authors.

CENTER TALK: READING

Canvas and Sam have just finished reading the book *Goldilocks and the Three Bears* by James Marshall (Puffin, 1998). They have been reading the book from memory, relying heavily on picture clues. Their teacher's questions invite them to explore characters and story structure.

TEACHER: Goldilocks sure seemed in a hurry to get out of there! What do you think she was most scared of?

CANVAS: That the bears would be mad at her for messing up their house.

SAM: They might eat her!

TEACHER: Do you think we could change this story so Goldilocks wouldn't be afraid?

CANVAS: Maybe you could make it so the three bears invited her in.

SAM: She'd still be scared.

TEACHER: What if the animals were changed to different kind of animals? What do you think might happen?

Writing Center

Todd is dictating a story to go with a picture he's drawn of himself and his friends playing soccer. He writes some of the letters, and the assistant helps with the rest. Nearby, Brennan and Diana are writing about the circus. Collaborating, they create a colorful poster announcing that the circus is coming to town. Kayla is busy outlining a story about rainbows and fairies (triggered by her interest in a movie she saw). She's using spelling approximations and pictures to communicate her ideas. Although these children are each working at a different level, they are all actively and purposely involved in writing.

Children often move from the art center to the writing center to write stories about their pictures.

Whether children are ready to learn about the sounds that letters make or using invented spellings to tell their own stories, the writing center is an ideal area to nurture all the facets of writing development at each child's level.

Writing Center Setup

The writing center is quite a large area of our classroom. The center's hub is a large round table—perfect for the discussion that literacy activities often involve. This setup encourages children to bounce ideas off each other and help each other with the mechanics of writing. Quiet areas are important, too. File

To avoid disruptions to instructional time, try to have all materials ready and available for children before school starts.

folders on one side of the table create study carrels. (Stand the file folders on the side to make a screen.) Other considerations include:

- Based on the need for both kinds of activities (collaborative and independent), the writing center works best when sandwiched between a quiet center and a louder one. Situate the area for quiet work on the side of the table near the quiet center, and the area for working conversations on the side next to the noisier center.

- Because the writing center is used so much, it is essential to restock supplies often, sometimes every day.
- Provide date stamps and stamp pads for children to use when they write in their journals. Each dated entry serves as concrete evidence of the child's progress—wonderful for sharing at conferences.

Supply List

In addition to pencils (large and small), pencil grips, pens, markers, crayons, colored pencils, and assorted papers, consider the following materials for a well-stocked writing center:

- ✓ pencil sharpeners
- ✓ envelopes
- ✓ stickers
- ✓ journals
- ✓ blank books
- ✓ notebooks
- ✓ rulers
- ✓ scissors
- ✓ stapler
- ✓ hole punch
- ✓ tape
- ✓ folders (for storing work)
- ✓ word banks
- ✓ word walls
- ✓ newspaper
- ✓ alphabet cards
- ✓ alphabet charts
- ✓ individual name cards and alphabet cards (laminated cards with each child's name and the letters of the alphabet)
- ✓ class list
- ✓ word cards to match labels around room
- ✓ junk mail
- ✓ chalkboard and chalk
- ✓ white board and markers
- ✓ letter stencils
- ✓ book-binding materials (brass fasteners, rings, pipe cleaners)
- ✓ clipboards
- ✓ waste basket
- ✓ typewriter
- ✓ computer and printer

Skills and Concepts

While at the writing center, children learn about the concepts of print and the alphabet. They begin to use prewriting and writing strategies, as well as drafting, revising, and publishing skills. They are experimenting with the conventions of print and the features and functions of language. Following are other important concepts children learn.

Work and Play

Parents often wonder what skills their children are developing during Choice Time activities, which often look like play. During Choice Time, I try to watch one or two children a day in particular. At the end of Choice Time, we fill out a form together stating all the areas of the classroom the child worked in (art center, reading center, and so on). Next, I write in the skills the child was working on at the particular centers. This lets parents know that play is a child's work, and it reinforces that we do teach skills in a developmental kindergarten. (For a reproducible of this form, see page 82.)

- prereading skills
- structural analysis
- sentence structure
- conventions of print
- language skills
- expressing feelings through writing
- story development
- organizational skills
- spelling
- editing skills
- fine motor skills
- handwriting skills
- speaking skills
- listening skills
- research methods
- experience with different genres
- imagination
- creativity
- problem solving
- care of materials

Modeling Literacy

Modeling is an important part of teaching literacy. While spending time at the writing center, take the opportunity to write while the children do. Watching adults write conveys the message that writing is rewarding and important work.

Emergent writing behaviors begin with random scribbling, proceed to more controlled scribbling, and later become scribbles which the children name. At the scribbling stage children may make a few scribbles on a page and tell you that they wrote their name. As time goes on, they begin to make close approximations to letters. These are the letters that float all over the page, bearing a slight resemblance to conventional letters. During this stage, children dictate their stories to adults, who assist in writing all or most of the letters.

Eventually, emergent writers will begin to write the letters of the alphabet, stringing these letters together in no certain order. These writers will be able to "read" what they wrote to you, and fully believe that you can read it as well. At this stage many letters will be reversed, or even tipped on their sides. As literacy skills develop, children will begin to use invented spellings. While young writers are continuing through this stage, adult help is still very present, but we begin to encourage the writers to write many of their own words. Detailed information on each stage of writing starts on page 112.

CENTER TALK: WRITING

Renee is making a birthday card for her dad. A conversation with her teacher helps her discover strategies she can use to read and spell unfamiliar words.

RENEE: *(Sounding out and spelling words)* H-A-P-E B-R-H-D-A D-A-D.

TEACHER: What are you making?

RENEE: A birthday card. Today is my dad's birthday.

TEACHER: Wow! That's great! Can I see?

RENEE: *(Shows the teacher the card.)*

TEACHER: Can you read it to me?

RENEE: *(Reading)* Happy birthday, Dad.

TEACHER: That's great! That's what I read, too. Hmm…birthday, birthday. That sounds like one of those tricky words that have two words in one.

RENEE: Oh! Like *today* when we do the calendar. It has the word *to* and the word *day* in it.

TEACHER: Right! How about *birthday*? What do you hear at the end of *birthday*?

CENTER STARTERS: ART, MATH, AND SCIENCE

Following the plans for the blocks, dramatic play, reading, and writing centers, use the information here to develop art, math, and science centers.

Art Center

Erin stands at the easel making her own version of "Starry Night" by Vincent van Gogh. She has been admiring the Van Gogh print hanging in the art center for some time, and has asked many questions during our discussions of famous artists. Leandro and Gus are busy gift-wrapping books they've recently made for their mothers. The art center is a bustle of creative activity that naturally lends itself to literacy opportunities such as reading, book-making, illustrating, and writing.

Children explore color and texture at the art easel.

The art center is generously stocked as needed before children arrive. This cuts down on interruptions later.

Setup: The art center works best if it is in an area that is large enough to accommodate one or two tables for working, as well as an easel or two. Of course, it's helpful to locate this center near a sink for easy cleanup. More suggestions include:

- It's a good idea to have a place to display children's work in the art center. If space is not available, set up a display elsewhere in the classroom.
- Set up the art center near the writing center to make it easy for children to move from one to the other as they write and illustrate stories.

JUST-RIGHT READ ALOUD

The Art Lesson by Tomie dePaola (Putnam, 1989): Young Tommy loves to draw. His teacher insists he use only school crayons, not his box of 64 beautiful colors. Later, Tommy and his art teacher strike a compromise. Pair this story with *Mouse Paint* by Ellen Stoll Walsh (Harcourt, 1989), a tale of three mischievous white mice who hide themselves from a cat on a sheet of white paper. When they find some paint, they can't resist experimenting with it!

• Cover easels with newspaper to keep them clean all year. When the newspaper gets soiled from paint, tear it off and start again!

• For quick cleanup, use wipe-off placemats as work mats. (Look for child-oriented mats with pictures on them, such as maps or the alphabet.)

Supplies: At the beginning of the year, I limit materials to a few basics, including crayons, colored pencils, different types of paper, markers, and scissors. Teach the use of crayons, and once children are using them carefully, make a big deal about opening a new box. Let each child choose one or two markers and crayons to add to the art

Rainbow paintings are typical of kindergartners' first works of art. Families and houses are often next.

center bin. This gives children a sense of ownership of materials and makes them eager to take care of them. Add play clay, glue, paint, and other materials as children learn proper use and care of the supplies. (See page 224 for play clay and paint recipes.)

Skills and Concepts: Children at this age process information while moving and standing, so creating at the easel is a perfect match. At this developmental stage, children like to draw things they see, making them as realistic as possible. Every year it amazes me to see the number of children who spend the first few months drawing the same pictures over and over, usually rainbows and houses. They like the feeling of competence that comes from drawing the same picture many times. As the year progresses, children naturally move from drawing their thoughts and experiences to writing about them. Important concepts children learn in the art center include patterning, spatial relations, fine and gross motor skills, classifying and sorting, prewriting strategies, beginning publishing, and the writing process.

Math Center

Elijah and Rhonda are working with pattern blocks today at the math center. They've made patterns on the floor, and patterns on pattern block cards. Bridget and Rick are busy jumping on a large number line that is attached to the floor. They practice counting by twos as they jump two spaces. Using movement and active involvement, they are constructing knowledge about multiples of two. Kindergarten chil-

As these boys build a marble race, they make predictions and test ideas.

dren are just waiting to try out their mathematical capabilities! Math center activities pique this natural interest and actively engage children in learning more. Math standards are easily met when a math center is well thought out.

Setup: To give children plenty of room to work with the manipulatives, locate this center in an area with ample floor space. This center tends to invite quite a lot of activity (which can also mean it's not as quiet as some), so try to situate it near the block and dramatic play centers, and away from the reading and writing centers. Up to four children in the math center at one time works well.

Supplies: Consider the following materials for a well-stocked math center: pattern blocks and cards, attribute blocks, Cuisenaire rods (small and jumbo), base ten blocks, Unifix cubes, number lines (small and floor size), number cubes, magnetic numerals with magnet board, shapes, geoboards, measuring tools (for standard and nonstandard measurement), calculators, clocks, a scale, tactile numbers and shapes, mirrors, playing cards, games (board and homemade), objects to count, graphs, egg cartons for sorting, and beads and string.

Skills and Concepts: As children explore the math center environment and materials, they investigate and examine questions, reason out solutions, and apply what they learn. For example, a child working with a marble race game might wonder, "What would happen if I left this bridge off? Would the marble keep rolling?" This child might test these ideas and begin to make inferences, which leads to the mathematical concept of generalization. The child can then make connections to other materials in the center, or to different areas of the classroom. In addition to the math skills and concepts outlined in the NCTM standards (see page 138), a math center offers opportunities in the following areas: sorting and classifying, hypothesizing, drawing conclusions, categorizing, using language and social skills, strengthening fine motor skills (including pincher control), experimenting with balance, and learning about care of materials.

Nonstandard Measurement

To give children practice with the NCTM nonstandard measurement strand, glue buttons, beans, or pennies to wooden craft sticks to make tools for nonstandard measurement. Let children measure items in the room with their sticks. This is great practice for reading a ruler later.

Science Center

As Tia and Brian check their baggie gardens, Tia exclaims, "The radish seed is growing!" Brian asks, "Why did you put a penny in your garden?

I don't think it will grow." Tia confidently replies, "Well, it might, haven't you ever heard of money trees?" Brian admits that he hasn't, but is rather excited about the prospect. They go to their journals and record their observations. At a science center, children are active learners, applying the scientific processes, making and checking hypotheses, and drawing conclusions. (Do pennies grow into money trees?)

With these indoor gardens, children can use their green thumbs and their data analysis skills all year.

Grow a Baggie Garden

To make a baggie garden, fold a paper towel into a small rectangle and soak it. Place the paper towel in the bottom of a large recloseable bag and put a row of staples through the bag, along the top of the paper towel. When children add seeds to the bag, the staples will help keep the seeds from falling into the wet paper towel, causing them to mold.

Setup: The science center works best near a window so children can observe the outdoors and have enough light for growing plants. Other considerations include the following:

• Shelving and counter top areas work well for storing larger materials and equipment, such as balance scales, pots for planting, clipboards, and an aquarium. Trays and cubbies are handy for storing smaller supplies, such as keys for sorting, seeds, magnifiers, and magnets.

• A sensory table is a great addition to a science center, and requires some room for children to explore. Try filling a sensory table with water, rice, dried corn, beans, bubbles, cornmeal, planting soil, pebbles, sand, shells, salt, Oobleck (cornstarch and water), gelatin, shaving cream, flubber (see recipe, page 224), and foam packing peanuts. Be creative and change the contents often!

Supplies: One way to keep the science center setup fresh and current is to include items that relate to the current season. Other materials to have on hand include recloseable bags, paper towels, science journals, keys (for sorting), seeds, potting soil, pots for planting (clear sides are great for observation), paper cups and plates, plastic containers with lids (such as film canisters), magnets, sand trays, scales (balance, bathroom), thermometer (indoor and outdoor), binoculars, clipboards, prisms, mirrors, magnifiers, measuring tools, microscope, and eye droppers.

Skills and Concepts: A science environment allows all children to learn and explore, no matter what their developmental level. As children engage in inquiry at a science center (whether they're counting acorns in a box or wondering why ice melts), they may be describing objects and events, asking questions, constructing and testing explanations, and communicating ideas. In the process, they build skills and concepts that include observing, comparing, classifying, communicating, measuring, inferring, predicting, collecting and recording data, interpreting, and making models.

Teacher's Choice

Once in a while I set up a "Teacher's Choice" center to highlight particular skills or concepts. I also use this center to offer materials that don't necessarily fit at other centers. Children love using the new materials and activities at these surprise centers.

TEACHER RESOURCES

Block Play: The Complete Guide to Learning and Playing with Blocks by Sharon MacDonald (Gryphon House, 2001): Here's all you ever wanted to know about block play, including how to explain it to parents.

Scaffolding Children's Learning: Vygotsky and Early Childhood Education by Laura E. Berk and Adam Winsler (National Association for the Education of Young Children, 1995): A must-have for anyone working with young children, this book offers the nuts and bolts of Vygotsky's theory on the development of children.

Science Surprises! Ready-to-Use Experiments & Activities for Young Learners by Jean Feldman (The Center for Applied Research in Education, 1995): Look for ideas that can be adapted for a science center.

Teaching Young Writers: Strategies That Work by Lola M. Schaefer (Scholastic, 2001): Practical advice and great teaching tips make this a useful resource.

A Year of Hands-on Science by Lynne Kepler (Scholastic, 1999): Two complete science units for each month feature activities, experiments, assessment tips, reproducible activity pages, and literacy connections. This book offers lots of ideas and inspiration for keeping a science center fresh and inviting all year!

Name _____ Date _____

What I Learned Today

Dear _____,

These are the areas of the room I worked in today:

_____

_____

_____

These are the skills I worked on today:

_____

_____

_____

Love,

_____

The New Kindergarten: Teaching Reading, Writing & More • Scholastic Professional Books

CHAPTER 6

Developing a Rich Reading Program

This morning Erin and Emily have chosen to spend some of their center time cuddling up with good books. The comfortable seating and warm lighting of the reading center make it an inviting place to explore books and other reading material. Erin and Emily start at the cover and the title page of their books. They announce the title, author, and publisher, and track the print with their fingers as they read each word—just like their teacher does during literacy time in the classroom!

From the time my students enter the classroom to the time they leave, literacy lessons are part of their kindergarten program. They're in the morning message that greets children each day and in the schedule that lets them know what the day will bring. They're in the songs that bring students together for their morning meeting, the mini-lessons that expand on the morning message, and the phonics games that teach letter-sound relationships. They're in center explorations that include reading for different purposes, read-aloud stories that children look forward to, pocket chart poems, class charts that children help create, labels around the classroom, and more. Even the daily closing circle makes literacy connections, bringing children together one more time to sing a song from a chart.

At the foundation of such a literacy-based environment is a teacher who understands each child and his or her level of development and cultural context. This chapter shows how to build on this understanding to create a literacy-rich environment that teaches essential skills in reading.

PHONICS INSTRUCTION

An important component (but certainly not the only component!) of the language arts curriculum is direct phonics instruction. In *Phonics from A to Z: A Practical Guide* (Scholastic, 1999), Wiley Blevins states: "Many children have difficulties with phonics instruction because they haven't developed the prerequisite phonemic awareness skills that other children gain through years of exposure to rhymes, songs, and being read to. Phonemic awareness training provides the foundation on which phonics instruction is built." In our classroom, we spend the first 25 to 50 percent of the school year playing with words in songs, charts, and books, and establishing phonemic awareness skills. When children have a solid understanding of word, sentence, and rhyme, I begin to teach phonics.

Teaching Phonics

Because phonics involves speaking and listening, it makes sense to teach it orally, and not with worksheets in an isolated environment.

A phonics lesson fits well with the morning meeting. During this time we explore the alphabet and I begin teaching letter sounds in a sequence. Each lesson incorporates oral language and models sounds for children, asking them to repeat the target sound. Five to ten minutes is about the right length for this lesson. (For sample morning meeting phonics lessons based on the morning message, see pages 34–35.)

Sound Sequence

The sequence of sounds taught depends on children's needs. Each lesson incorporates a review of previous lessons as well. In a typical year I start by teaching consonant sounds that I have targeted according to the unit we are studying. (For more information on targeting letters for thematic study see the Tip on page 181.)

I begin with consonants that appear frequently in words that the children will be using during shared reading, interactive writing, and the reading of classroom charts and songs. Letters I typically cover first include *d, t, m, h,* and *s,* as they lend themselves well to making short vowel-consonant-vowel words. I then introduce vowel sounds, focusing on short sounds and always making mention that the long sound of vowels "say their name." Usually I begin with the letters *a* and *e* because of the frequency with which they appear in text. I always teach *q* and *u* together. Introducing common consonant sounds and short vowel sounds allows children to start putting together short words that they can read, motivating them to learn more sounds and interact with print on a regular basis.

After children have learned the vowel and consonant sounds, I introduce digraphs such as *wh, th, sh,* and *ch.* If children are ready, I may teach some blends, but often I teach these skills in the context of literacy lessons throughout the day and only to individual children who are ready for this next step. I make sure to incorporate all target sounds/letters into the morning message and share Big Books, poetry, and song charts that include the targeted sounds so that children have many opportunities to use their skills within a meaningful context.

Skill-Building Songs and Games

For years, parents and educators and other childcare givers have known that playing language games and singing songs enhances children's vocabulary and instills in them a wonder about language. Kindergarten

Keep in Mind...

Jim Trelease calls reading an "accrued skill" and goes on to report that "students who read the most, read the best, achieve the most, and stay in school the longest."

—from *The Read-Aloud Handbook* by Jim Trelease (Penguin, 2001)

is the ideal environment for these playful approaches to literacy. Following are games to play, and activities to use with songs.

Games to Play

In addition to the literacy activities described in the previous section on morning meeting/morning message (see pages 33–37), here are six quick and easy games for reinforcing phonics lessons. Play them at the morning meeting. Allow about five to ten minutes for these mini-lessons.

Buzz! Write each letter of the alphabet on an index card. Write the word *Buzz* and draw a

Playing with language like the words to this favorite Maurice Sendak rhyme *(Chicken Soup With Rice)* is one of the best ways to build strong readers.

picture of a bee on four or five additional cards. Shuffle and stack the cards. Gather children in a circle, take the first card from the stack, hold it up, and say the letter (the sound, too, if children are ready, and later, a word that starts with that letter). If you select a Buzz card, everyone gets up, buzzes around like a bee, and sits down. Pass the stack of cards to the child next to you, and have that child repeat the process. As children play, they build letter recognition, listening, and oral language skills.

While playing Buzz!, this boy demonstrates his knowledge of the letter *o*.

CLOTHESLINE WORDS: Make several tagboard cutouts for each letter of the alphabet. Divide the cards into consonant cards and vowel cards. Display a consonant letter on a clothesline (at children's eye level). Say the letter name and its sound. Invite a child to choose a vowel sound to hang with this letter, and another child to hang another consonant sound at the end. Each time a child adds a letter, say the letter name and its sound. The object of the game is to create consonant-vowel-consonant words. You may want to limit the letters children can choose from to include only those you've taught. *Variation:* Children hold up word cards in order instead of hanging them on a clothesline.

ADD A BEGINNING: Write a word ending on a sentence strip (such as -*at*). Place the strip in a pocket chart. Invite children to take turns adding different beginnings to make new words (*sat, bat, rat, mat,* and so on).

WHAT'S MY WORD? Children love to play this variation of the old game Hangman. On chart paper, write three dashes to represent the letters in a consonant-vowel-consonant word, such as *cat*. Let children take turns guessing letters. Record correct guesses in the appropriate places and write incorrect guesses to the side. Have an alphabet chart visible to help children make their choices. Make the words more difficult as children's skills improve.

IN THE BAG: After teaching a letter and sound, give each child a bag on which you've written the target letter. Invite children to scour the room for items that start with that sound and place the items in their bags. Bring children together to share their findings. Record the words on chart paper. Read the list together, letting children take turns using a pointer to highlight the target letter in the words that go with their items. Then let children return everything to its place.

SECRET LETTER: Make letter necklaces by cutting out each letter of the alphabet from tagboard and stringing it on yarn. Give each child a necklace to wear. Have children find an object in the classroom that starts with their letter, and place it in a bag to hide it. Let children

A bag holds a surprise that teaches letter-sound relationships.

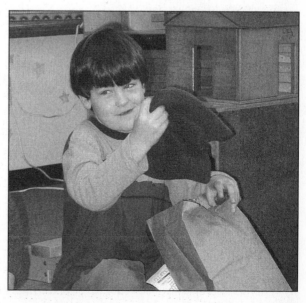

take turns standing in front of the class, naming their letter, and telling the sound it makes. Then have them give three clues to help classmates guess what's in the bag. Allow students three guesses before the child reveals the contents. Children love this game, and it supports social interaction and oral language in the classroom. *Variation:* Let children wear their necklaces home. Have them find an item at home that starts with their letter and, with parents' permission, bring it to school (hidden in a bag). Continue playing as above.

Songs to Sing

Children still love the old kindergarten classics, such as "The Farmer in the Dell," "London Bridge," and "A-Tisket, A-Tasket." These songs have a game component, making them perfect for literacy-building lessons. New songs can have the same playful quality. The wonderful by-product in either case is that children enjoy the songs so much, they want to repeat them again and again. Here are several ways to weave songs into the day and build literacy at the same time.

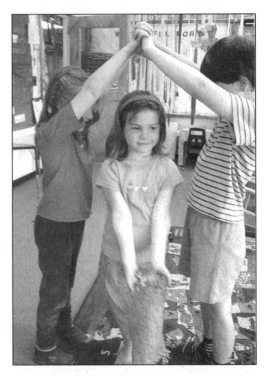

Songs like "London Bridge" combine movement with oral language. Write the words on chart paper to encourage children to match the words they sing to print.

Song Resources

Other songs with game-like appeal include "BINGO" and "Old MacDonald Had a Farm." The library is a great resource for locating songs and games you may vaguely remember from childhood. Children also know songs that the rest of the class may not be familiar with. When children are given the opportunity to teach songs they know, it boosts their self-esteem and broadens the scope for all children (and for the teacher!). Parents are often happy to share songs that they know, too.

MOVE ALONG: Songs that incorporate movement are a perfect choice for young children. "Head, Shoulders, Knees, and Toes" is a favorite. Use it to teach names for parts of the body at the same time. Label an outline of a child's body on chart paper with the parts mentioned in the song.

THIS IS THE WAY: Invite children to help make up new verses to "The Mulberry Bush." For example, in place of "This is the way we wash our clothes," sing "This is the way we line up for lunch," or "This is the way we get on our coats." Write new verses on chart paper to revisit throughout the year.

THEME SONGS: Look for songs to go with themes you are teaching. For example, "Down by the Station" is fun for a transportation theme. "The Itsy, Bitsy Spider" will bring a unit on creepy crawlies alive.

TRANSITION TIMES: Play a favorite song during transitions. Write the song on chart paper to read and sing at the morning meeting. Children will quickly learn the words through repetition, building word recognition and vocabulary.

SING AN ALPHABET SONG: Alphabet songs make learning about letters fun. *ABC Sing-Along Flip Chart and Tape* (Scholastic, 2001) features 26 fun songs, each of which builds phonemic awareness through irresistible lyrics set to favorite tunes.

HOME-SCHOOL CONNECTIONS: Parents often remember the songs you use from their childhood, and they make a nice home-school connection for children to share with their parents. Photocopy some of the old favorites to send home with children. Families will enjoy singing them together. You might suggest they store song sheets in a binder or folder to enjoy again and again.

Everyone's a Reader!

When children come to kindergarten, I call them all readers. They may be "reading" a song that they know from memory from a chart. They may be retelling a story in a book as they look at pictures. When I say that they "read" the morning message, I mean that each child is "reading" it at his or her current developmental stage.

A KINDERGARTEN READING PROGRAM

The desire to read is key to reading success. We must make children burn to read stories on their own. We need to fill their days with literature that they can relate to and that makes them want to pick up books again and again. In kindergarten there are many opportunities for children to discover the joy of reading. Most children love to hear a story; we need to capture that desire and make it a powerful drive for them. I like to expose children to many different genres and forms of literature. We read charts and songs, poetry, fairy tales, chapter books, and magazines. It's important that reading is incorporated into every part of the kindergarten day. Reading builds vocabulary, and the larger the vocabulary children have, the better they

Read alouds are a favorite part of the day.

Book Frenzies

During literacy time the children in my classroom like to choose a favorite book, or a book recently checked out of the library, and have a "book frenzy." To have a book frenzy, ask children to gather in a circle with their chosen books. Say "Pass," and have them give their books to the classmate next to them. Give children enough time to become familiar with the new book (so they want to pick it up later, on their own), then call out "Pass" again. Have children repeat this until the books have gone all the way around the circle.

are able to understand concepts. Here are several routines you can build into your day to spark your students' love of reading, including pocket chart poems, book frenzies, read alouds, shared reading, and book clubs. You'll also find detailed information about the stages of reading your students might be at, and how you can meet their needs at these various levels.

Read Alouds

Reading aloud is the cornerstone of the kindergarten curriculum. Following are strategies for reading aloud picture books with kindergartners:

- Create a warm, cozy atmosphere for read alouds by turning off the overhead lights and turning on small lamps.
- Choose stories that you enjoy. Children pick up on your feelings, even if you don't have the best acting abilities!
- Be sure to preview the story before reading it to children.
- During the settling down time, before you start to read the story, invite children to make predictions.
- State the book's title, author, publisher, city where it was published, and date it was published. Kindergartners love this information;

If each day we read just two picture books aloud to children, we would add 360 books to their repertoire. Three books a day and we would add 540 books. This is a significant contribution to each child's vocabulary.

conversations about how long a story has been around or where a book was published are often generated. It's fun to find the place of publication on a map, too!

- Share related information with children. This might be something you know about the author or the making of a book, background information on a story or character, or news about an award. For example, I always share stories about Tomie dePaola with children when I read one of his books; they think it's great to know that he loves popcorn and cats.

- If needed, preview vocabulary children might need to know. In order to increase children's vocabularies, unfamiliar words must be explained, not simply read.

- Find the setting of the story on a map or, if it is known, the place where the author lives.

- Hold the book so all children can easily see the pictures; it helps to sit just a little above children while reading.

- Use expression and different voices as you read. Be sure to read slowly enough; often we rush through a book without realizing it.

- Allow children to fill in words or chant along with predictable text.

- Reread books, especially favorites!

Combining read alouds with activities extends children's understanding. Here are several favorite read alouds and activities to use with them. There are many sources of additional book-based activities. (For some ideas, see page 102.)

The Important Book by Margaret Wise Brown, illustrated by Leonard Weisgard (HarperTrophy, 1990): I read this book as part of a culminating activity for many of the thematic units we study. For example, after a unit on community helpers we read this book, and then make a class book entitled *The Important Book About Community Helpers*. Each child writes about a particular community helper using *The Important Book* as a model: "The important thing about police officers is they keep us safe. Police officers direct traffic, help us cross the street, and visit our schools, but the most important thing about police officers is they keep us safe."

The Doorbell Rang by Pat Hutchins (Greenwillow, 1986): We often make cookies together after sharing this story, and then act it out using the real cookies. We experiment with different ways to divide the

Chapter Book Read Alouds

Young children are often ready to hear chapter books long before they would ever be able to read them. Reading chapter books to kindergarten children increases their vocabulary, improves attention span, and cultivates complex thinking. Some favorites are:

- Newbery Honor winner *Charlotte's Web* by E.B. White (HarperCollins, 1952)
- *The Littles* by John Peterson (Scholastic, 1993)
- *James and the Giant Peach* by Roald Dahl (Knopf, 1961)
- *Pippi Longstocking* by Astrid Lindgren (Viking Press, 1950)
- *Ramona the Pest* by Beverly Cleary (Morrow, 1968)
- *Stuart Little* by E. B. White (HarperCollins, 1945)

Keep in Mind...

"The single most important activity for building the knowledge required for eventual success in reading is reading aloud to children."

—from *Becoming a Nation of Readers* by Richard C. Anderson, Elfrieda H. Hiebert, Judith A. Scott and Ian A.G. Wilkinson (Center for the Study of Reading, 1985)

cookies, and make sure everyone has one cookie at the end. Children love this and could do it again and again!

Cinder-Elly by Frances Minters (Puffin, 1997): Use this and other fairy tales to make butcher-paper story maps. Use interactive writing to have children determine the beginning, middle, and end. Write these parts of the story across a large sheet of craft paper, and have children illustrate each section. Display the illustrated story map. Children will enjoy using it to retell the story on their own. As a variation, let each child make a smaller story map. (For a story map template, see page 103.)

The True Story of the Three Little Pigs by John Scieszka, illustrated by Lane Smith (Viking, 1989) and ***The Three Little Pigs*** (several authors and versions): After reading *The Three Little Pigs* and *The True Story of the Three Little Pigs,* discuss the different viewpoints of the pigs and the wolf. What do wolves like to eat? Could there have been a misunderstanding or lack of communication between the pigs and the wolf? Using interactive writing (see page 116), make up a new story about the three pigs and the wolf. Encourage children to take different points of view. For example, maybe the wolf was making his famous berry pie to enter in the county fair when he needed to borrow a cup of flour from his neighbors, the pigs. He began to sneeze when the flour tickled his nose and…. Be sure to leave space on each page for children to illustrate the story.

Illustrated story maps help children retell stories in sequence.

With shared reading experiences, children can interact with text at their own level.

Shared Reading

Shared reading is the next step in the read-aloud process. I add this to literacy time about six weeks into the school year, when children are more focused. Shared reading stems from Don Holdaway's development of a "Natural Learning Classroom Model." In this model, Holdaway includes *demonstration, participation, practice/role play,* and *performance.* Through these four parts of the process, children engage in the text—reading along, exploring words, playing with language, and enjoying the success of putting their new skills to work on their own.

During shared reading, I demonstrate reading by reading aloud a Big Book or chart. (The large type makes it easy for children to interact with the text.) Children are then invited to participate by reading along, masking words (see page 35), and asking questions. Children build on their knowledge of the story during Choice Time, when they might dramatize the story, reread the book, write their own version, and so on. Children continue with the process, reading aloud a favorite song or chart, reading a book to the teacher, or publishing a written piece of work.

When I choose a Big Book for a shared reading experience, I like to start with books that have predictable text, which naturally engages children. As time goes on and children become more familiar with the shared reading format, I include books of different genres and some classic folk tales, such as "Goldilocks and the Three Bears" and "Little Red Riding Hood." Although these books do not offer predictable text, they are usually quite familiar to children, who enjoy chiming in or acting out the stories on subsequent readings.

Stories for Shared Reading

More predictable books for shared reading are:

- *Brown Bear, Brown Bear, What Do You See?* by Bill Martin, Jr. (Henry Holt & Co., 1996)
- *Chicken Soup With Rice* by Maurice Sendak (HarperCollins, 1962)
- *It Looked Like Spilt Milk* by Charles G. Shaw (HarperCollins, 1993)
- *Mrs. Wishy-Washy* by Joy Cowley (Philomel, 1999)
- *The Very Hungry Caterpillar* by Eric Carle (Putnam, 1983)

Keep in Mind...

"Increasing the volume of children's playful, stimulating experiences with good books is associated with accelerated growth in reading competence."

—from *Learning to Read and Write: Developmentally Appropriate Practices for Young Children* by Susan B. Neuman, Carol Copple, and Sue Bredekamp (National Association for the Education of Young Children, 2000)

Especially for Half-Day Kindergarten

Any time children are working on more independent work, gather a book club together. Choice Time is one option. Book clubs don't need to meet every day.

Children quickly decide which Big Books are their favorites, and we read them again and again. To deepen children's understanding each time, I change an element of the shared reading experience. For example, I might ask children to fill in words and phrases on repeated readings, or to use different tones of voice as they chime in. If a text is one that can be sung, children love to read the words in the first reading, and sing it in other readings. The large print lends itself to masking activities, in which children can find and mask target words. Often we act out some of our favorite stories during repeated readings.

Book Clubs

In the beginning of the year during Choice Time, I spend a lot of time watching children and taking copious anecdotal notes. I want to get a sense of each child's experiences with print and their literacy abilities, because it's important for me to know how familiar they are with books. This is a very informal time when children read to me and I read to them. Most children love having this reading time with the teacher all to themselves, and soon they are vying for my attention. When this starts to happen, I post a sign-up sheet for reading to the teacher.

This informal time together, sharing the joy of books and print, is crucial to setting the stage for the school year. I want children to feel comfortable with books, and to enjoy reading. I want them to see me enjoying books and discussing stories. I want them to know that books are fun and are valued in our classroom.

You can send a book club off to work on their own from time to time, with brief check-ins with you.

As I spend this informal time reading with and to the children, I begin to see different reading stages emerge. There are many different ways to label the stages of reading. I've come up with labels that work for my classroom. The most important aspect of any label is that it is used to indicate a particular developmental stage, not to permanently label a child. Children need to be met at their own developmental level and should be challenged to work at the edge of their developing capacities.

As the particular reading stages start to take shape, I begin to plan what I call "book clubs." Usually I have about three clubs working at any one time during Choice Time. One club works on alphabet activities, another club includes emergent readers, and sometimes I have a club for early readers. Occasionally, I have children who are reading at levels beyond these reading stages, and I create individual plans for them and include them in groups from time to time. (For reproducible checklists of the skills at each of these levels, see pages 104–107.)

Shared Literacy Experiences With Children

I usually have a copy of a book I am reading on my desk at school. The book might be related to education, and I'll share with children some new ideas for our classroom. Other times this book might inspire students' own learning goals. For example, when I read *In the Heart of the Sea: The Tragedy of the Whaleship Essex,* by Nathaniel Philbrick (Penguin, 2001), I shared the whaling stories with children. Since we live on Martha's Vineyard, my students could really relate to the information, and we added a study of whales to our ocean unit.

Skills Checklist for the
Alphabet Awareness Stage, p. 104

Skills Checklist for the
Emergent Reading Stage, p. 105

Skills Checklist for the
Early Reading Stage, p.106

Skills Checklist for the
Transitional Reading Stage, p. 107

The book club groups are adjusted as needed, depending on individual needs and how a group is working. Most groups meet for about 15 to 20 minutes on most days. As readers become more fluent, I may only check in with them during their club time, and work independently with individuals as needed. Each decision is based on group and individual needs.

Providing time in the day for book clubs gives children opportunities to:

- Experience literacy in a social setting, promoting oral language.
- Develop appropriate skills for their individual level.
- Match spoken word to written word.
- Explore patterns of language.
- Discover all aspects of books (spaces between words, letters, words, sentences, top and bottom of page, left-right directionality of print).
- Notice new words and increase their vocabulary.
- Strengthen their phonemic awareness skills.
- Learn about story structure.
- Explore different genres.
- Use self-correcting and self-monitoring skills while reading.
- Use all forms of decoding skills (picture clues, context clues, structure clues, reading for meaning and understanding).
- Explore the way print works.
- Build a sight-word vocabulary.

Book Club Activities: Alphabet Awareness

Teaching the alphabet is crucial to the overall success of literacy learners. Children at this stage benefit from activities that allow them to manipulate letters and play with language. Following are a few of the activities that children in my class enjoy while working in a book club at this level.

ADDING-MACHINE-TAPE LETTERS: Give children a long piece of adding machine tape. Have them use rubber alphabet stamps to stamp out the letters of the alphabet in order. Alphabet friezes offer assistance to children as needed.

LIMA-BEAN LETTERS: Write each letter of the alphabet on a lima bean. Let children match these letters with the adding-machine-tape letters. Children can also use the lima-bean letters to spell their names and other words.

Sorting small toys by the first letter of their names strengthens alphabet skills.

THE TOY GAME: Write each letter of the alphabet on a clean take-out container (available in craft stores) or another small container. Gather a collection of small toys in a basket. Let children sort the toys into the containers according to the first letter of the toy's name.

ADD-A-LETTER ALPHABET BOOKS: For each new letter children learn, have them make a page for an alphabet book. For example, a child who is learning about the letter *s* would write the letter *s* on the page and might decorate it with *sponge* painting. Letter *r* might be decorated with *rainbow* colors. Label the illustration that goes with each letter. At the end of the school year, each child will have an alphabet book to take home.

Book Club Activities: Emergent Reading Stage

Children at this stage need a lot of practice with predictable and simple texts. They are becoming more familiar with print each day, making more and more connections to print. Following are a few of the activities that children in my class enjoy while working in a book club at this level.

MATCHING WORDS TO PRINT: Start by having children draw a picture of something they want to write about. Invite them to dictate stories about their pictures. Write their exact words on the paper. Then type the same words into the computer and print them out.

Scheduling Book Clubs

I run book clubs during Choice Time, pulling children into their groups for activities related to the book they're sharing.

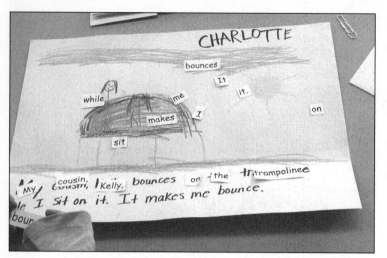

Children match computer-printed words to stories they dictate to build numerous reading skills.

Cut up these words and give them to students. Have them match the computer-printed words to the print on their pictures. They can then read their stories, pushing up the computer-printed words as they read each one. Then have students isolate certain words, mix them up again and reread, pushing up the words along the way. This helps children build a sight-word bank, promotes tracking, and reinforces the concept of one-to-one correspondence.

NURSERY RHYMES: Nursery rhymes are great to use with emergent readers, as many children are familiar with them. Nursery rhymes are also a rich source of rhythm and rhyme, adding to phonemic awareness skills. Read a nursery rhyme and then write it on small sentence strips. Place the sentence strips in a small pocket chart. Give children their own copy of the nursery rhyme cut into small sentence strips. Let them match their sentence strips with those in the pocket chart.

SHAPE STORIES: After reading and discussing a familiar book, ask children to identify the main events in the story. Cut craft paper into several shapes that match the story. (For example, for *The Three Little Pigs*, cut out pig shapes.) Revisit the story with children, recording events in the story on the shapes. When the retelling is complete, let children help sequence the shapes and bind them to make a shape book. As a variation, leave the pages unbound and place them at a literacy center. Ask children to put them in order as they read the story. (They might look at the book that goes with them at the same time.)

Book Club Activities: Early Reading Stage

Children at this stage of reading are having success with predictable and familiar texts. They are able to use several strategies to decode words, such as using visual, meaning, and structural cues. They are beginning to try reading books that have not been read to them by adults. They need to have time to read books and explore print on their own, as well as in book clubs. Following are a few of the activities that children in my class enjoy while working in a book club at this level.

UNIFIX CUBE WORDS: Write letters on Unifix cubes. Give each child several cubes that spell words using phonograms you are working on (*-at, -all,* and so on). Say a word that you would like children to spell, for example, *cat.* Ask children to repeat the word and then spell it with the cubes, saying each sound and touching each letter as they spell it.

WORD FAMILY FLIP BOOKS: Have children write a word family ending at the end of a four-inch sentence strip. Have them write various onsets for this ending on sentence strips cut into two-inch pieces. Stack the onsets on top of the blank part of the ending and bind to make word family flip books.

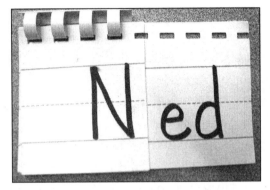

Word family flip books help children learn to blend words.

CLASSMATE CONCENTRATION: Play a game that helps children learn to spell each other's names. Laminate children's photos on index cards (one photo per card) and write their names on a second set of cards. Turn the photo and name cards face down. Let children take turns turning the cards over two at a time to try to make a match. Play the same game with sight-word cards. (Write each word on two cards.)

Sarah

Matching names to classmates' photos makes a fun reading center activity.

Becoming Fluent Readers

As young readers move from the transitional reading stage to fluency, they will:

- Self-monitor their reading.
- Read for meaning and purpose.
- Read from a variety of genres for a variety of reasons.
- Use background knowledge and knowledge of how print works to decode unfamiliar words.
- Have a large bank of sight words.
- Have increased vocabularies.
- Change the pace of their reading as needed for the type of reading (newspaper, novel, textbook).
- Refer to text to support ideas.
- Read for pleasure.
- Synthesize the information read.
- Integrate all reading strategies.

EXTENDING A PATTERN: Using a favorite story, song, poem, or rhyme, ask children to extend the pattern to include their own ideas. One of my favorite books to use with this activity is the book *Honey I Love* by Eloise Greenfield (HarperTrophy, 1986). I type out the phrase "Honey I love _____" on several pages and ask children to make a book about the things they love.

Book Club Activities: Transitional Reading Stage

During this phase of reading, children's reading ability increases a great deal. They are finding out that print can be used for many purposes. They are reading fairly independently and can extend their learning with activities after a book is read. Many children in kindergarten do not reach this level in reading. For children who do reach this level in kindergarten, we need to keep in mind their developmental and emotional level and their need for play. Following are some book club projects and activities for children at this level.

BOOK CLUB JOURNAL: If there is more than one student in this reading level, they can eventually run their own book club. Provide guidelines in journal form to keep children focused. (For a reproducible journal, see page 108.) Have children keep a list of the titles they read.

AUTHOR STUDIES: Author studies give children a chance to learn more about favorite authors and their styles of writing. This activity also encourages children to read more books by authors they like, and then to compare and contrast stories. For example, if children are reading the Clifford books by Norman Bridwell, give them a large template of a big red dog. Let them record things they discover about Clifford on the template with each book they read.

NONFICTION STUDIES: I like to encourage children at this level to read nonfiction books to learn more about a theme we are studying. Children love using templates in corresponding shapes to record information. For example, if the theme is Ocean Life, they can record facts on a fish-shaped paper.

READING AND THE HOME-SCHOOL CONNECTION

I once heard someone say that the only things required for success in reading were a library card and a bed lamp for reading. This really makes sense to me. But many families do not use the public library, and may not have extra money to purchase books for their homes. Yet it is critical that children have books in their homes to look at, read, and have read to them. Here are some ways to build children's at-home libraries and their exposure to books:

BOOK BAGS: Each Monday, pack up several books for each child—some that children can read independently, and others that parents can read with them—in a large recloseable bag. There are no assignments; the only goal is that children and their families enjoy the books together. (See page 110 for a Book Bags send-home letter.)

LITERACY KITS: Team up with colleagues to put together several literacy kits to send home with children on a rotating basis. To make a kit, stock a sturdy bag with a book and related activities for children to do with their families. Add a puppet or a toy character from a book if possible. These kits should give families several activities to choose from, so that they can tailor the fun to their own interests and desires.

READ IT AND KEEP IT: Set aside a special shelf for books children can keep—when they can read them. (Purchase the books at yard sales, flea markets, and so on.) When children can read one of these books to you, let them take it home. This is a real motivator for children, and a cost-effective way to get books into children's homes.

BOOK GIFT CERTIFICATES: Why spend money on junky toys and candy for children, when you could just as easily spend it on books? Many of the book clubs (such as Scholastic, Trumpet, and Troll) offer gift certificates, which I give as holiday and end-of-the year gifts. When our PTO had a surplus of money from a fundraiser, they gave each child in the school a gift certificate to the local bookstore.

BIRTHDAY BOOKS: Instead of having a box of birthday toys for children to choose from, why not let them choose from a book box? Obtain books inexpensively through book club bonus points or at yard sales.

Send-Home Pages

Families appreciate information that will help them encourage learning at home. For a send-home letter on read alouds, see page 109.

BOOK SWAPS AND SALES: Our school holds a "Food for Thought" book sale each year. Families donate used children's books, which are displayed in flea-market fashion. Children are then asked to bring in a can or box of food or a quarter to purchase a book. The food and money goes to the local food pantry. Another alternative is to have families bring in used books and swap them for "new" ones.

BOOK CLUB ORDERS: Sending home a monthly book club order gives families opportunities to purchase inexpensive books. Book clubs also offer bonus points which can be used to purchase books for the classroom library or as gifts and incentives for children.

TEACHER RESOURCES

The Beginning Reading Handbook: Strategies for Success by Gail Heald-Taylor (Heinemann, 2001): This outstanding resource includes information on organizing the classroom for literacy learning, and on communicating with parents.

Guided Reading: Making It Work by Mary Browning Schulman and Carleen DaCruz Payne (Scholastic, 2000): The booklist is a wonderful tool for matching books to readers. This resource also has some nice emergent reading assessments.

Phonics from A to Z: A Practical Guide by Wiley Blevins (Scholastic, 1999): This resource includes more than 100 phonemic awareness, alphabet recognition, and phonics activities.

The Read-Aloud Handbook by Jim Trelease (Penguin Books, 2001): Newly revised, this favorite still has all of its classic appeal. The booklists are an outstanding resource.

Teaching for Comprehension in Reading, Grades K-2 by Gay Su Pinnell and Patricia Scharer (Scholastic, 2003). This resource discusses the strategies and structures readers need to comprehend text—and the changes readers experience as they move up the primary grades.

Teaching With Favorite Leo Lionni Books by Kathleen M. Hollenbeck (Scholastic, 1999): Use the timeless tales of this beloved author to strengthen skills in reading and more. Other books in the series include *Teaching With Favorite Clifford*® *Books*, *Teaching With Favorite Franklin Books*, *Teaching With Favorite Kevin Henkes Books*, *Teaching With Favorite Patricia Polacco Books*, *Teaching With Favorite Dr. Seuss Books* (December, 2003), and *Teaching With Favorite Eric Carle Books*.

Name _____ Date _____ Book Title _____

Story Map

Characters:

Setting:

Beginning:

Middle:

End:

Name _____ Date _____

Alphabet Awareness Stage Checklist

Children at the Alphabet Awareness Stage:

___ Recognize the letters in their name and a few other letters.

___ Can say or sing the alphabet.

___ Recognize some environmental print.

___ Have some knowledge of the purpose of print.

___ Can write their name.

___ Enjoy hearing books read aloud.

___ Will pretend to read a familiar book.

Name _____ Date _____

Emergent Reading Stage Checklist

Children at the Emergent Reading Stage:

___ Are beginning to understand how print works.

___ Know that print is talk written down.

___ Rely on picture clues as they read predictable and simple texts (text with approximately one line of print per page).

___ Know a few sight words.

___ Retell stories that have been read to them (often memorized).

___ Begin to recognize familiar words.

___ Know the reason for spaces between words.

___ Begin to notice first letters of words.

___ Start to know the difference between a letter and a word.

___ Are beginning to use some one-to-one correspondence.

___ Use prior knowledge to make a connection to the story.

Name _____   Date _____

Early Reading Stage Checklist

Children at the Early Reading Stage:

___ Are able to demonstrate one-to-one matching of words.

___ Notice beginning and ending sounds of words.

___ Still rely on pictures, but do so less and less as they begin to use visual, meaning, and structural cues.

___ Are better able to control their eyes as they read, and are not as apt to point to words as they read.

___ Use meaning to decode words and understand the text.

___ Self-correct.

___ Notice familiar words in unfamiliar text.

___ Use prior knowledge to make sense of their reading.

___ Read slowly and deliberately.

The New Kindergarten: Teaching Reading, Writing & More • Scholastic Professional Books

Name _____ Date _____

Transitional Reading Stage Checklist

Children at the Transitional Reading Stage:

___ Have increased reading ability.

___ Have deeper understandings of books they have read and books that are read to them. (They understand characters, endings, and story structures better.)

___ Make predictions and check them during reading.

___ Have a large sight-word vocabulary.

___ Read punctuation marks appropriately.

___ Choose to read a variety of books and genres for different purposes (to gather information, for enjoyment, etc.).

___ Decode words based on a variety of strategies (using meaning, grapho-phonic clues, context clues, and structural clues).

___ Self-correct and self-monitor their reading.

___ Read books that are more text-dense.

___ Do not need to rely on picture clues as much.

___ Read fluently with some expression, most of the time.

Name _____ Date _____

Book Club Journal

Club Members: _____

_____

_____

_____

Book Title: _____

Author: _____

Illustrator: _____

_____ We looked at the pictures.
_____ We read the story, taking turns.
_____ We talked about the story.
_____ We chose a new book to read for our next meeting.

Color in the face to show how you
feel about the way your club
worked together.

Write a sentence.

_____

_____

The New Kindergarten: Teaching Reading, Writing & More • Scholastic Professional Books

Name _____ Date _____

Reading at Home

Dear Families,

Did you know that there is a direct correlation between the number of books read to a child and the child's reading success? Reading aloud to your child is one of the best ways to help your child become a strong reader. Here are some other reasons to read aloud to your child:

• To let your child see literacy skills modeled by family members.

• To positively reinforce literacy skills learned in school.

• To build vocabulary.

• To foster imagination and creativity.

• To enjoy books together and build a warm relationship with each other.

• To build background knowledge.

• To instill a love of lifelong learning.

As you read aloud to your child, keep these tips in mind:

1. Try to read aloud with your child every day.

2. Establish a regular time for reading together. Turn off the television and radio.

3. Share some of your own favorite children's books with your child.

4. Visit the library and help your child look for books that reflect special interests.

5. Remember that listening is a skill that is strengthened the more children are read to. You may want to increase the number of minutes you spend reading with your child each day to reflect these growing skills.

6. If you are reading a longer book to your child and need to break it into segments, always stop at a suspenseful part. You'll both look forward to returning to the story the next time.

7. Talk with your child about what you are reading. Discuss predictions for what will happen next in the story.

8. Vary your reading pace according to the story. (Slow down for suspenseful parts—go ahead and be dramatic!)

9. Respond to your child's questions about the book. You can ask what your child thinks, and share your own ideas.

10. Enjoy the books and the time spent together!

Name _____ Date _____

Book Bags

Dear Families,

Enclosed in this bag you will find _____ books that your child has chosen (with teacher assistance) to read this week. Children learn to read by looking at books, being read to, and attempting to read by looking at pictures and "playing" with words. Please take time this week to help your child with these books. Read these books with your child, letting your child join in on familiar or predictable words. Enclosed you will also find a bookmark that shares more tips for reading with your child.

Please return the books and the bag to the classroom on _____. Your child will continue to bring home a book bag each _____, which will need to be returned to school the following _____.

I hope you enjoy reading these books with your child! Have fun!

Sincerely,

Reading Together

❀ Turn the pages slowly to give your child time to look at the pictures. Answer questions your child has along the way.

❀ If your child is reading a story and comes to an unknown word, it's okay to say it and let your child continue. Too many interruptions can interfere with your child's enjoyment and understanding of the story.

❀ Whether your child is listening to you read, "reading" pictures, or reading words, be sure to communicate how much you enjoyed your book time together. Your enthusiasm will encourage your child's interest in reading.

The New Kindergarten: Teaching Reading, Writing & More • Scholastic Professional Books

CHAPTER 7

Developing An Effective Writing Program

oday the room is humming with the sound of busy writers. Emily is at the writing center, binding her book with help from a classroom volunteer. When it's done she beams, "My mom and dad will love this! Now they can see everything I do at school!" She begins reading the book she made as she points to the pictures and words. She is a budding author and so proud! This is the kind of literacy experience that spurs a child on to reading and writing on a regular basis.

Most children are curious about writing. They have watched adults write, and wonder about the process of writing. What are those funny lines and squiggles stretching across the paper? When we, as kindergarten teachers, provide an environment that fosters the love of learning and a wonder about words and writing, we can hook children into discovering and enjoying the writing process. This chapter includes an overview of the stages of writing in a kindergarten classroom, and writing approaches and activities for strengthening skills through group and individual work.

WRITING STAGES

Most children enter kindergarten somewhere around the prewriting to emergent writing stages. They've been exposed to some print, and are becoming curious about writing. I like to spend time individually with each child early in the school year to ascertain which stage of writing they are at. When I am familiar with each child's writing level, I can tailor my writing instruction to each individual child. Following is a list of behaviors usually associated with each stage of writing in kindergarten.

Prewriters

Children who are in the prewriting stage of writing development draw pictures and use scribbling to write. When asked about the print and scribbles, children at this stage will often indicate that the picture they drew has nothing to do with the scribbles they wrote. Letter formation is inconsistent and print is written in any direction. The prewriting stage is characterized by stages of scribbling and writing that most children go through before they enter kindergarten. Characteristics of this stage include:

RANDOM SCRIBBLING: Children are experimenting with writing tools, beginning to see that the tools make marks on the paper. They have very little control of the pencil at this stage, and are holding the pencil fisted in their hand.

CONTROLLED SCRIBBLING: As their muscle control develops, children tend to repeat patterns. Often a child will make circular scribbles over and over again, or draw a series of lines. Pencil grip is still fisted.

SCRIBBLING WITH A PURPOSE: During this stage, children will explain what they have drawn. For example, many children at this stage draw pictures of their families. Each person is often characterized as having a head and two long legs coming straight from the head. When asked, the child will name the family members. Pencil grip may start to be a little more refined at this stage, depending on the amount of exposure that the child has had to writing.

The long legs in this picture of a child's family are characteristic of a prewriter.

RANDOM FORMS: Children begin to make letter-like drawings. They tend to appear all over the page in random order. Children pretend to write with these letters, at times separating the letters from the drawings.

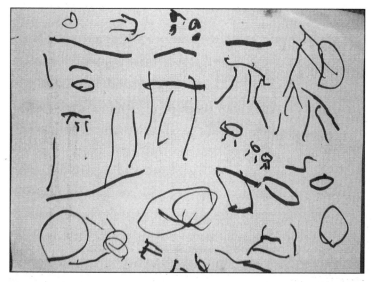

These random forms will soon lead to letters.

RANDOM LETTERS: Children at this stage use a random string of letters in any direction. They "read" their writing and believe others can, too. Children show many reversals during this stage, and their letter formation is inconsistent. Children at this stage will write their name and begin to copy print. Pencil grip is becoming more controlled and conventional.

Early writers use some of their own words and copy others.

Early Writers

Early writers are beginning to take more risks with writing. They begin to notice more conventions of print and start to have an understanding of the alphabet. Kindergartners in the early stage of writing development typically do the following:

- Draw pictures to represent their thoughts.
- Understand (and most times will demonstrate) that print is written from left to right.
- Understand that writing is talk written down.
- "Read" their own writing.
- Use one letter to represent a word, usually an initial consonant.
- Begin to show some sound-to-letter correspondence.
- Inconsistently use spacing between words and letters.
- Begin to label pictures.
- May randomly use punctuation.
- Begin to take more risks in writing.
- Begin to choose their own topics for writing.

Emergent writers experiment with writing more words on their own.

Emergent Writers

As writers gain more practice and confidence at writing, they begin to emerge into conventional writing. Kindergartners in the emergent stage of writing development typically do the following:

- Draw pictures that match their story.
- Use approximations in writing.
- Use most consonant sounds (at least beginning and final sounds), and some vowel sounds in their writing.
- Use many high-frequency words.
- Begin to demonstrate a story plan using beginning, middle, and end.
- May randomly use periods in their writing.

Uppercase and lowercase letters are evident in this more fluent writer's story.

Fluent Writers

In kindergarten, young writers get lots of exposure to print and lots of practice with writing. As the year continues, children become better writers, and some reach the fluent stage of writing for kindergarten. Kindergartners in the fluent stage of writing development typically do the following:

• Draw detailed pictures that are relevant to the topic.
• Use details in stories that run throughout the piece of writing.
• Consistently use spaces between words.
• Use some punctuation, and period placement is consistent.
• Correctly spell some high-frequency words.
• Begin to use uppercase and lowercase letters appropriately.

WHOLE-GROUP WRITING ACTIVITIES

There are three types of writing that are typically used as a whole-group writing experience with children who are at different stages of writing development: language-experience writing, shared writing, and interactive writing. Following is an overview of each, and a more detailed plan for interactive writing, which is a primary tool for writing instruction.

Keep in Mind...

"In many homes and schools, 3-, 4-, and 5-year-olds are told to 'stay within the lines' when writing letters and numbers. Empirical evidence shows that most young children cannot successfully comply with this request....They get frustrated, cry, and start developing a negative attitude toward writing in general. This is because they first need to practice sweeping strokes by painting and writing large letters with thick brushes, pencils, felt tip pens, or chalk. Writing at the chalkboard, or on unlined paper, or at an art easel, is the best preparation for eventually being able to 'stay within the lines.'"

—from *What's Best for Kids* by Anthony J. Coletta (Modern Learning Press, 1991)

We froze three³ pans of ice. We made predictions about what would melt ice faster. On one pan of ice we put water and salt. On one pan of ice we put water. On another pan of ice we put salt. We made a graph of our predictions. Most people thought water and salt would melt the ice the fastest. We found out that the ice with just salt on it melted faster.

A language-experience writing activity lets all children contribute, regardless of the words they know how to write.

Language-Experience Writing

In language-experience writings, the teacher acts as a scribe to record children's ideas. Language-experience writings are usually written after a class activity, such as a field trip or science experiment. The language-experience approach works well with kindergartners, because the words they use are more elaborate than what they are typically ready to read and write themselves.

Shared Writing

Shared writings are similar to language-experience writings, except that during shared writing the children's attention is focused more on the composing of the text. The teacher still acts as a scribe for the children, however. As you try to help them think of the best way to put their thoughts on paper, you may give suggestions and guide them in the planning process of the writing more than you would during a language-experience writing. My students often create shared writings based on books we have read. We may follow the pattern of a favorite book as we construct our own text. (See sample, right.)

D is for diving at Stale Beach. Kids dive off the bridge into the water. KEVON

When we were studying our community, I used the book *M Is for Mayflower: A Massachusetts Alphabet* by Margot Theis Raven (Discover America State by State Alphabet Series, Sleeping Bear Press, October 2002) as a spinoff for our own book. Here's a page for the letter *d*.

Interactive Writing

I tend to use interactive writing quite a bit because it incorporates many of the shared writing strategies that help to build literacy skills, but also allows children to share the pen with the teacher, directly contributing to the writing. During interactive writing I focus on goals I have for children and their writing. Each child is called on to share the pen based on goals I have for that child. For example, if I know a child is becoming familiar with a particular word family, I will ask that child to use the pen to write that pattern in a word. Because I want to include all children, I may call some children up to fill in the letter that begins their name. Each time I call a child to the easel to share the pen, it is for a specific purpose and based on that

An interactive writing approach makes it easy to tailor each part of the process to children's individual goals.

child's developmental writing level. This writing will be shared and read by members of the classroom, so I strive to have conventional spellings, letter formations, and punctuation in the piece of writing.

Throughout an interactive writing lesson, the children and I share a running dialogue about the topic, conventions of language, and the plan and voice for writing. Mini-lessons are embedded in each lesson, providing opportunities for each child to grow as a writer. Following are how-tos for introducing an interactive writing session covering writing, reading, and reviewing the piece.

Stage 1: Prewriting

Each interactive writing session starts with a meaningful reason to write. It might evolve from a shared book, poem, or song, an experience such as a field trip, a guest speaker, or an activity in the classroom. It could also come from an individual child's experience, if the class agrees to write about it. My class has written about problems that arose in class and how they were resolved.

A discussion about the writing then takes place: What type of writing does this particular experience call for? A letter? A list? A

Interactive Writing Materials

Have the following materials on hand in the large-group area of the classroom:

- An easel (tall enough for all children to see as they sit on the floor, but not so tall that reading the print creates neck strain)
- Large-lined chart paper
- Markers of different colors
- Correction pens, scraps of paper, and mailing labels for making corrections

fictional story? A work of nonfiction? What voice should the piece be written in? This is the time that the class focuses on the composing process. We might develop a web, a list, or an outline during this part of the interactive writing process to help direct the writing. Mini-lessons such as the following samples can help children understand how adults often get started writing.

STORY ORGANIZER: This activity helps children when writing a piece of fiction or other piece of writing told in story form. Give children a large sheet of construction paper and have them fold it "hot dog" style (horizontally). They now have two flaps of paper folded together. On the top flap have them make two cuts to create three sections of paper that can be lifted up to reveal the paper underneath. On the first flap have them write the word "beginning," on the second flap "middle," and on the last flap "end." They then lift each flap and draw and write about each part of the story to organize their thoughts. (See sample at left and template, page 130.)

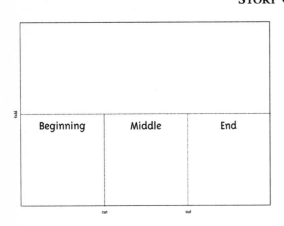

WEBBING: Using large chart paper, begin to make a web by recording the writing topic in the center. Ask children to help you think of areas they would like to include under the topic. Record ideas to create a web.

CONSTRUCTING A STORY: Have children tell you details they want to include in a story. Help them organize their ideas on paper in order (from first to last). Label each sentence with a number to indicate the order it should appear in the piece of writing.

Stage 2: Writing

This is the actual writing of the piece, in which the teacher and children share the pen. As children are helping to construct the text, they are also learning how print works: They see the directional movement of print; letters, words, and sentences; and spaces between words. As words are spelled out, they are learning the sounds that letters make to form words. As the class composes and writes together, you take the role of expert writer, leading and encouraging the group, all the while sharing the pen with the students. It is crucial to keep in mind the desired skills during each interactive writing lesson.

During this writing, you explicitly teach skills to the children. Following are tips to keep in mind during this stage:

- Don't feel that every child must have a turn with the pen for every interactive writing lesson, but do try to be sensitive to children's desires to help.
- Tell children what you are doing and why at each step of the interactive writing process.
- Point out interesting words and parts of words (the features of language).
- Use children's background knowledge to help them write.
- Have children stretch the words as they say them. (See "Stretch It," below.)
- Use standard writing conventions.
- Remember that oral language is crucial to the interactive writing process.

The possibilities for mini-lessons at this stage are endless, and must be based on each class, and each individual child within the class. Some mini-lessons that I have found effective in my classroom are:

STRETCH IT: Pronounce a word very slowly, holding each sound for a few seconds. Ask children to carefully watch your mouth as you say the word. Next, use a rubber band or a Slinky to stretch the sounds as you say them. Ask children to say the word with you very slowly. When children are trying to figure out how to spell a word, give them the Slinky or rubber band and ask them to stretch the sounds before writing them.

PHONICS PHONE: These are phones made from PVC pipe. They are shaped like a telephone receiver and have an opening at the ear and mouth. Children speak into the phone, and the word projects into their ear, making the sounds extremely clear. These phones help children identify sounds in speech. For ordering information, call the CANDL Foundation at (800) 633-7212 or go to www.PhonicsPhone.org.

WORDS HAVE SHAPES: Encourage children to notice the shapes of words. For example, the word *bed* really looks like a bed. The word *look* has two eyes. To help children notice the shapes of words, use large highlighting tape cut to the shape and size of words. Hold up a shape cut from highlighting tape and ask students to identify a word with that shape. Chart masks can also be used for this activity.

The Daily News

At the end of each day, my class gathers for one last time and writes the daily news together, using either shared writing or interactive writing, depending on the time of the school year. Writing the daily news helps children review their day and gives them a purpose for writing. I start the year by using shared writing with the students, simply recording their responses, and as the year continues I begin to share the pen with the students. After the daily news is written, I type it and the children illustrate it the next day. It is then bound in a book for children to revisit, serving as a diary of our school year.

Magnetic Writing Boards

Have children use magnetic writing boards (such as MagnaDoodle) to practice writing words before adding them to a piece of interactive writing.

Revisions

As the text is reread, consider portions that may need revising (although I would caution against changing the overall message). Help children practice what they know about phonics, spelling, and word families to address spelling errors.

Stage 3: Reading

After the message has been collaboratively written, it is important to read it over together for clarity. This models an important skill needed in the writing process: reading a passage to check the writing. The rereading should take place at different points during the writing, but certainly after the message is completely constructed. During the rereading you can revisit lessons and skills learned during the writing phase, and ask children about the different features of the text as they are reading it.

While rereading the text, use the pointer to demonstrate one-to-one correspondence of written word to spoken word. This helps children learn a sense of space with words, and understand that words can have more than one syllable. Tweak words, spellings, and punctuation as needed. Mini-lessons to use during the reading stage include:

SOUND-WORD CORRESPONDENCE: Ask children to use beautiful pointers of any sort (wands work great) to point to the words as the class reads them. Have children hold the pointer on each word until the whole word is spoken. Teach syllabication in words as opportunities arise. With practice, children become expert pointers, which helps their sound-word correspondence.

COUNTING SYLLABLES: While rereading, ask children to clap each syllable to identify the sounds. This helps them learn to read and spell new words.

Stage 4: Reviewing

During the reviewing stage of interactive writing, the teacher explicitly teaches the intended concepts. A piece of interactive writing can be reviewed over and over again. I like to review a piece immediately after we write and read it. Sometimes children ask to revisit favorite pieces of writing days or weeks later, and that makes for great review as well. Reviewing is an excellent time to point out to children exactly what it is they learned during the writing lesson. Reviewing is a great time to ask children to notice certain functions and features of language. Highlighting tape, pointers, reading masks, and Wikki Stix are all great tools to use as they isolate parts of the writing. Some of the mini-lessons I use at this stage are:

WORD FAMILIES: Keep charts of word families and after reading a piece of writing, search for words to add to these lists. This helps children notice similarities and differences in words.

RHYMING WORDS: Find a word in the passage and try to think of a word that rhymes with it. This can be turned into a game, with each child trying to come up with a rhyming word.

MATCHING WORDS: Write a word in the text on a sticky note and ask children to place the sticky note over the word it matches.

JOURNAL WRITING

Writing and reading together as a group at morning meeting and literacy time gives children multiple experiences with print. Journal writing gives children a chance to experiment with some of the skills they've been learning during these group activities. Journal writing provides opportunities for children to:

- Develop an interest in writing.
- Learn the customs of writing.
- Practice writing skills.
- Sequence thoughts.
- Experience the feeling of having something important to write.
- Experiment with the functions, features, and patterns of language.
- Use left-to-right progression of words.
- Practice letter formation.
- Experiment with punctuation and capitalization.
- Build phonemic awareness.
- Understand the importance of spacing between words.
- Use and see standard spellings.
- Take risks in writing.

Storing Journals

I use a hanging file basket (found at office supply stores) and hanging files to store the children's journals—as well as individual dictionaries and any other writing—alphabetically by first name. These are kept in the writing center for easy access.

Journals provide a wonderful record over the year of children's growth as writers.

Assessing Student Writing

Use a date stamp for children to stamp each page of their journal, so you can easily see on which date a child was demonstrating certain writing behaviors.

We become writers by writing; to see the most growth in children's writing, they should write often. I strive to have children write in their journals each day. I often teach a prewriting mini-lesson to help them get started. I might talk about a personal story that I want to write about, and model the process of writing it for the children. Sometimes I'll talk about a book I've read, or one we've read in class, and I'll write about that. I want children to know that they can write about many things in their journals. A list of possible topics can be helpful for children who find the "openness" of a journal daunting. This section explains the plan I follow for using journals in my classroom (based on the stages children move through), as well as suggestions for special journals and assessment strategies.

Stage 1: The Beginning of Journal Writing

When school begins, my students find blank journals to use in the writing center. These first journals are simply made from five blank sheets of unlined paper stapled between construction-paper covers. The journals are purposely short in length at the beginning for quick completion and success. Children are very excited about their first journals and want to take them home quickly. At this time, journals are not discussed at any real length, and they are not a part of the daily requirements. They are available for children to use (or not) as they wish. There is no pressure.

During this time, I am reading lots of literature that grabs children's interest and holds it. I want children to be excited about words, and to wonder how to write words down as the authors of stories do. Children are enjoying writing stories and accounts of events together during literacy time, and I begin to encourage them to create their own during Choice Time. This informal time, in which children are settling into the classroom and becoming interested in language, is the beginning of journal writing. Generally, this period lasts from three to six weeks, depending on the group of children.

A class volunteer supports a young writer in the beginning stages of journal writing.

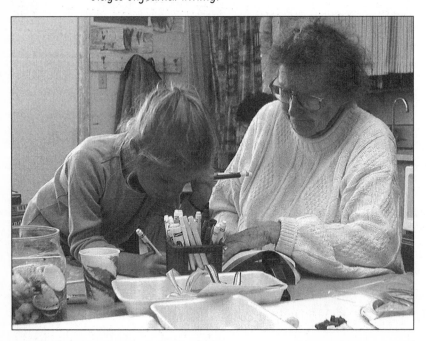

Stage 2: Journal Drawings

After children have had the opportunity to pick up journals on their own and have had many group writing experiences, I begin to ask them to draw pictures in journals. Many children also choose to write words about their pictures. I believe it is important to teach drawing pictures for journals to some degree in kindergarten. I want children to know that I expect their best work when drawing pictures, and guide them as needed in using several colors, filling the page, and adding details. During literacy time, I draw pictures for children

Children are encouraged to use detail in their journal drawings. This detail will carry over into the stories they write or dictate.

and we talk about what makes a picture fun to look at. Exploring illustrations in picture books inspires children to hone their own journal drawings. Although we continually work to improve artwork all year, this particular stage of journal writing lasts approximately three to six weeks, depending on the group of children. After children are drawing pictures to the best of their abilities we move into writing in the journals as a requirement.

Stage 3: Drawing and Writing

During this stage, children are required to write in journals, usually each day. They start by drawing pictures to convey meaning. Some choose to write words on their own, which is encouraged but not required. Others will ask an adult to take dictation of a story that goes with a picture. At this time, the children who are eager to learn how to write their own words will begin to surface. If I feel they are able to write their own words I will encourage them, helping them sound out words they are trying to spell. As such needs present themselves, I begin individual mini-lessons to encourage each child's writing development.

Stage 4: Dictating Journal Stories

After children have had some experience drawing pictures in their journals and some have started to write or dictate their own words, I begin to

TiP

Mini-Lesson Topics

Mini-lesson topics that work with each of the three beginning stages of journal writing include:

- Finding writing journals in the hanging file basket and replacing them.
- Locating writing tools and replacing them in the appropriate spot.
- Coloring pictures using at least five colors.
- Using details in drawings.
- Labeling pictures with beginning consonants.
- Conferencing with the teacher and classmates.
- Using environmental print and the word wall for spelling.

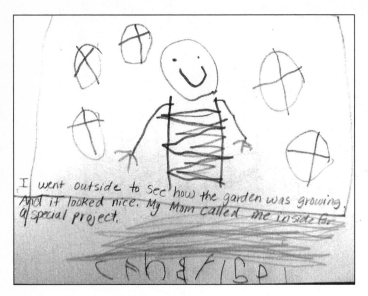

I went outside to see how the garden was growing. And it looked nice. My Mom called me inside for a special project.

Having students dictate stories to go with their pictures builds writing vocabulary and helps them to become more comfortable with independent writing.

Taking Dictation

Keep a dialogue going during dictation to help children make connections between letters and sounds. For example, I may notice that a child is on the cusp of writing words, so I will talk about the beginning consonant of each word as I write it.

require that they dictate a story to go with each picture they draw. I require this dictation for approximately four to six weeks, or until each child is ready to move on to writing their own words. I make journals for this stage with 15 to 20 pages that include a box for a picture and lines for dictation. I continue to use this type of paper in the journals for the remainder of the school year, but as the year continues, some children may have a smaller box for a picture and more lines for writing, based on their writing development. (For reproducible journal pages, see pages 131 and 132.)

Stage 5: Writing

This stage in journal writing lasts through the end of the year. Children continue to improve upon their entries, adding more details, improving the story line, and writing their own words. Some children, of course, are not ready for writing their own words, and they will continue through the appropriate stages as they are developmentally ready for them.

During this stage of journal writing, children are also asked to reflect on their work as they complete journals. When children complete a journal, they are given a form that asks them to look over their work, finding specific pieces they are proud of or would like to improve. (See reproducible, page 133.) They then take this paper home with their journal and ask their parents to look over their journals with them and comment.

Keeping Journal Writing Fresh and Fun

Introduce special journals periodically to keep journal writing fresh. Some ideas for special journal projects are:

Official Reports: Children can share news about their day with you, reporting on incidents in writing rather than in speech.

Loose Tooth Journal: Make tooth-shaped pages for this fun journal.

The Boo-Boo Journal: Bandage-shaped pages invite children to tell about their many mishaps.

Reading Response Journals: Practice responding, in some way, to a shared book by writing about it together. Later, include it as a journal assignment.

Alphabet Journals:

Staple 26 pages together to make this journal. Write a letter of the alphabet at the top of each page. Invite children to draw five pictures of items that begin with each letter as it is introduced in a lesson. They then dictate the word to an adult, who writes the word for them.

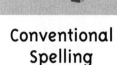

An alphabet journal makes a fun and informative spelling resource.

Spelling Considerations

I encourage children to try to spell words themselves first. However, I do not want them to become frustrated and give up. It's a juggling act, trying to teach just enough to help a child along, but not so much that the child loses interest. Spelling aids that work well in kindergarten include word walls, personal dictionaries, and "Have a Go" spelling sheets.

Word walls are popular in kindergarten, and can be added to as children learn more words. Word walls are best used if they are at the children's eye level. I use library pockets with a word card in it, so the word can physically be carried to the table where the child is writing. Many children are not developmentally ready to copy words directly from a word wall, and need the word directly in front of them.

When a child reaches a level where there is a constant need to know how to spell words that are not readily available in the classroom, a personal spelling dictionary may work well. This is a paperback book with several words listed under each letter, and blanks to add new words children learn how to spell. There are several types of these dictionaries commercially available. Children who are eager to learn conventional spellings do very well with these dictionaries, and they reach new levels of writing independence.

TiP

Conventional Spelling

Many educators believe that any writing done by children should be accepted by their teacher. I agree with this to some degree, but believe it is important for children to see conventional spellings of words they are writing. For this reason, while the child reads a journal passage aloud, I use a very light pencil to write conventional spellings beneath words that are spelled phonetically.

125

Assessing Journal Writing

I use children's writing journals and a writing rubric to assess writing development four times a year (November, January, April, and June). I circle the behaviors on the writing rubric, and wherever the most writing behaviors lie, that is the stage of writing development I ascribe to that individual child. Using writing journals for assessment is authentic and gives a clear picture of a child's writing development. (For a reproducible writing rubric, see page 135.)

"Have a Go" sheets are simple forms on which children record words in one column that they want to know how to spell. The teacher checks the spelling and circles all the letters that are correct. The child tries to spell the word again in a second column. Again the teacher circles the correct letters. Finally the child or the teacher writes the standard spelling. (For a reproducible "Have a Go" sheet, see page 134.)

Name Kristen		Date 5/7	
Have a Go			
Copy Word	Try 1	Try 2	Standard Spelling
RBIT	RABIT	RABBIT	RABBIT

WRITING AND THE HOME-SCHOOL CONNECTION

Parents are the first and most important teachers of their children. Children learn by example when they see their parents write. Sometimes parents are intimidated by writing with their children, believing their own writing must be perfect before they can share it with their children. We need to encourage parents to write with their children, and let them know that writing takes many forms—from writing recipes, letters, lists, and messages left on family message boards to notes written to teachers. When I read journal and magazine articles, or books that I think will help parents support their children's writing skills, I make sure parents get a copy. Other ways to help parents teach their children to write and to inform them about the writing process include:

LITERACY NIGHT: Invite parents into the classroom for a relaxed and informal meeting about literacy learning in kindergarten. Discuss the developmental stages of writing and demonstrate some of the pieces of the writing program, such as interactive writing. The conversation will almost always move to spelling. Share spelling aids, such as word walls, and explain how children can be encouraged in their use of standard spelling. Parents leave such a meeting feeling more comfortable with the writing program, and more knowledgeable about encouraging their children's writing efforts at home.

CLASSROOM NEWSLETTERS: Newsletters are a nice place to offer quick tips for writing. Share information in question-and-answer form, by developmental stages, or by various topics about writing.

PEN PALS: Invite parents to send in some self-addressed, stamped envelopes for children to write to a family pen pal, such as a grandparent or far-away family friend. Writing to a pen pal is a big writing motivator for children. An added bonus is that it enhances important relationships.

E-MAIL: Children think it is so neat to e-mail their parents from the classroom computer, and the response from parents is often quick. This is a great way to use technology!

AUTHOR'S BRIEFCASE: This is an old briefcase that is packed full of writing supplies for children to take home on a rotating basis. Parents love it,

E-mailing family members from school creates meaningful reasons to write and read.

because children stay so busy with the briefcase when they bring it home. It also gives parents new ideas for literacy and writing projects they can do with their child. Some of the things to include are: pens, pencils, markers of all types, crayons, tape, stapler and staples, assorted papers, highlighting tape, scissors, stickers, blank cards, shaped notepads, labels, sentence strips, sticky notes, hole punches, and anything else that is interesting to use with writing activities!

Send-Home Pages

Page 136 features tips for strengthening writing skills at home. Photocopy this page and send it home with students or make it available at open-school night.

SHARED JOURNALS: Shared journals are used for children and parents to maintain a correspondence. These are not used every day, but as the child or parent wishes. Children write notes to their parents and carry them home, and the parents respond. Sometimes I ask children to write in their shared journals for a particular reason, such as asking to bring something into school the next day.

TRAVEL JOURNALS: Encourage parents to have their children keep a journal while they are traveling. They can include pictures, drawings, and other pieces of memorabilia. With new scrapbooking stores cropping up everywhere, accessories for a travel journal or scrapbook are easy to find.

Travel journals assure that children continue writing and reading while they're on vacation.

TEACHER RESOURCES

Fresh Takes on Using Journals to Teach Beginning Writers by Jim Henry (Scholastic Professional Books, 1999): A classroom teacher shares tips, strategies, and activities for using journal writing as a steppingstone for other kinds of writing. Though intended for grades 1 and 2, this resource will be helpful for encouraging kindergartners who are at a fluent stage of writing. (See page 115.)

Learning to Read and Write: Developmentally Appropriate Practices for Young Children by Susan B. Neuman, Carol Copple, and Sue Bredekamp (National Association for the Education of Young Children, 2000): Information on research is combined with developmentally appropriate practices for literacy teaching in early childhood.

Let's Write: A Practical Guide to Teaching Writing in the Early Grades by Mary Dill and Nancy Areglado (Scholastic Professional Books, 1999): A principal and classroom teacher share fresh ideas for setting up an effective writing program in the kindergarten, first- and second-grade classroom.

Literacy Through Play by Gretchen Owocki (Heinemann, 1999): This includes a play-based plan for setting up developmentally appropriate environments for literacy learning.

Make Way for Literacy! Teaching the Way Young Children Learn by Gretchen Owocki (Heinemann, 2001): This informative book shows how to support literacy learning in a developmentally appropriate classroom, and includes some wonderful books to encourage emergent literacy.

Reading and Writing in Kindergarten: A Practical Guide by Rosalie Franzese (Scholastic Professional Books, 2002): Young children benefit from a playful approach to learning. The material in this book recognizes that approach while also meeting instructional needs through read alouds, shared reading, guided reading, interactive writing, and other lessons.

fold

Story Organizer

Beginning

cut

Middle

cut

End

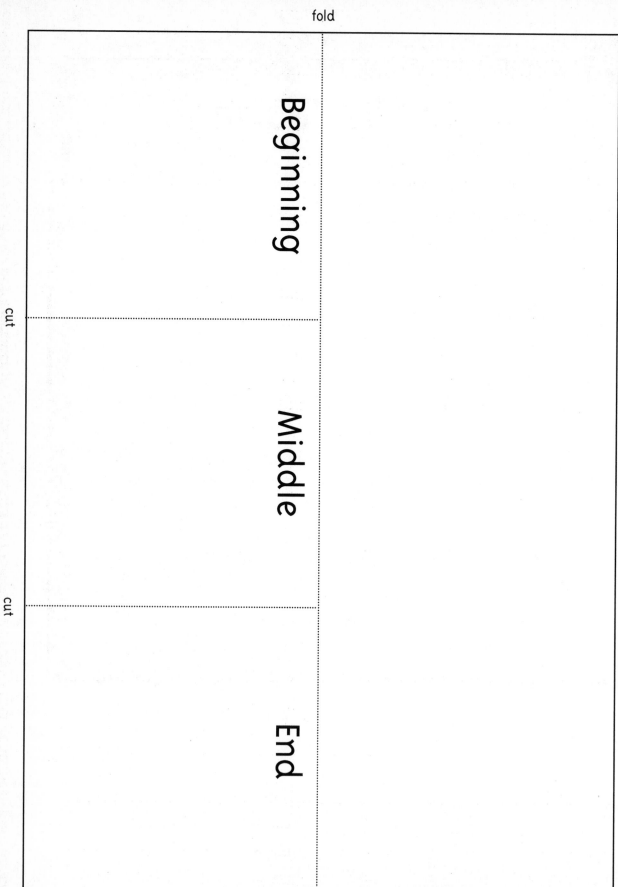

The New Kindergarten: Teaching Reading, Writing & More • Scholastic Professional Books

Name _____ Date _____

Journal Page

_____

_____

_____

Name _____ Date _____

Journal Page

The New Kindergarten: Teaching Reading, Writing & More • Scholastic Professional Books

Name _____ Date _____

Journal Reflection Page

Dear _____ ,

As you look at my journal with me, I would like you to notice:

I am working on: _____

These are things I do well: _____

_____

My favorite page is: _____

because: _____

_____

Please use the back of this paper to comment about my journal.

Love,

_____

Name _____ Date _____

Have a Go

Copy Word	Try 1	Try 2	Standard Spelling

The New Kindergarten: Teaching Reading, Writing & More • Scholastic Professional Books

Name _____

Date _____

Kindergarten Writing Rubric

WRITING STAGE	CONTENT	UNDERSTANDING OF PRINT	CONVENTIONS OF PRINT	SPELLING
FLUENT WRITER	• Uses detailed writings and drawings outlining events in the story. • Uses details that build upon each other throughout the writing.	• Consistently uses spaces between words. • Writes recognizable sentences. • Print is written left-to-right on the page.	• Uses uppercase and lowercase letters appropriately most of the time. • Uses some punctuation. • Period placement is consistent.	• Correctly spells some high-frequency words. • Each speech sound is represented in words.
EMERGENT WRITER	• Draws pictures that match story. • Begins to show a beginning, middle, and end to story. • Uses details in the story.	• Uses spaces between words most of the time. • Print is written left-to-right on the page.	• Uses uppercase and lowercase letters inconsistently. • Randomly uses periods, sometimes as ending punctuation.	• Uses beginning and ending consonant sounds. • Uses some consonant sounds found in the middle of words. • Uses some vowel sounds. • Uses approximations in spelling.
EARLY WRITER	• Draws pictures with little detail to represent thoughts. • Begins to label pictures with words.	• Uses spaces between words inconsistently. • Writing is random, found all over the page. • Some copied words beginning to appear.	• Uses uppercase letters. • Randomly uses punctuation.	• Uses one letter to represent a word, usually a consonant.
PREWRITER	• Draws to convey meaning. • Dictation/writing does not always match drawing.	• Uses strings of letters. • Writing is random, found all over the page.	• Scribbles. • Inconsistent letter formation. • Punctuation is not used.	• Writes own name. • Writes letters, but with no sound-to-letter correspondence.

Name _____ Date _____

Writing at Home

Dear Families,

You can help build your child's writing skills at home with the following activities. Keep in mind that some kindergartners are just learning about letters, while others are forming words. Please provide support for any of these activities at your child's level. For example, if your child is learning to recognize letters, you might use the magnetic letters in the first activity to spell your child's name together, saying and pointing to each letter in order. If your child is using some letters to spell words, you might write the conventional spellings underneath your child's words to reinforce sound-to-letter correspondence. Most of all, have fun with your child to encourage more writing at home!

Magnetic Letter Writing Board

Cover a cookie sheet with colored contact paper (or leave it plain) and give your child magnetic letters to experiment with making words. This is a great activity to take along on a car trip. (Start with the letters in your child's name. Your child may also like to try making words that appear on street signs, stores, and so on.)

"Painting" Words on Pavement

On warm days give your child a bucket of water and a paintbrush. Let your child "paint" words on a safe, supervised paved outdoor area. Variation: Let your child use sidewalk chalk to write words.

Grocery List Maker

Post a pad of paper on the refrigerator. When your family runs out of something, invite your child to add it to the paper to make a grocery list. (You can write conventional spellings beneath your child's words.) Let your child read back the items on the list as it grows.

Order Form Fill-Ins

Remove order forms from catalogs you don't need. Let your child practice filling in parts of them, such as the name line and the number of items.

The New Kindergarten: Teaching Reading, Writing & More • Scholastic Professional Books

CHAPTER 8

Meeting the
Math Standards

Children are immersed in mathematics from an early age and come to school with a good informal understanding of mathematics. Many children know the difference between more and less, larger and smaller, and have some idea about counting and number operations. Of course, these terms are the formal terms for math operations, whereas children can be heard verbalizing these understandings in ways such as: "Renee has three candies and I have only two! She has more than I do!" or "We're going to make it fair and share; let's cut the cookie in half, so we'll both have the same amount."

Using the experiences that children bring to the classroom, I strive to teach mathematics in as natural a way as possible. I want children to know that math is a part of our life every day, and that we are all problem solvers and mathematical thinkers. This chapter includes a look at the expectations for a kindergarten math program, and features a framework for meeting the standards through Choice Time exploration, literature-based mini-lessons, math time lessons, thematic units, everyday activities, and home-school connections.

ABOUT THE MATH STANDARDS

The National Council of Teachers of Mathematics (NCTM) originally formulated mathematics standards in 1989. Since then they have been revised a few times. The newest document was published in 2000 and now includes prekindergarten as well as grades kindergarten through 12. These standards are called Principles and Standards for School Mathematics, and include ten process and content standards for prekindergarten through second grade. These are Number and Operations, Geometry, Algebra, Measurement, Data Analysis and Probability, Problem Solving, Reasoning and Proof, Communications, Connections, and Representation. The math time section in this chapter includes a list of standards that match each sample lesson and activity. (See pages 148–153. Additional activities to support specific standards appear on pages 153–156.)

TEACHING MATH WITH EVERYDAY ACTIVITIES

Much of the math that is taught in our kindergarten classroom is not part of the scheduled math time. It happens when the manipulatives

Time For Math!

There are two signs in our classroom that tell children when math time will take place. The first is during the morning meeting, where the schedule for the day is posted. The second is a song that serves as a transition to math: "Number Rock" by Greg and Steve (from *We All Live Together, Volume 2*, Little House Music, 1978). Children love this jazzy song, which introduces the concept of counting to 20 in an active and fun way.

won't fit back into the box they were taken out of, when there aren't enough blocks to build the last turret on the castle, and when we need to make a decision about how to rearrange recess on the day of a special event. Here are suggestions for using opportunites such as these to strengthen math skills.

Problem Solving

Problem-solving opportunities arise every day in the kindergarten classroom—when there are not enough scissors for everyone at the art table, when children do not come in from the playground when called, or when the classroom rabbit has chewed everything in sight. Such situations provide authentic opportunities for problem solving. Letting children figure out their own answers facilitates natural mathematics learning. As children problem solve, adults can give them the time needed to arrive at an answer and ask questions to facilitate planning, strategic thinking, and reflection. As the year progresses, children will become better thinkers and self-sufficient members of the learning community.

Transition Time

Transition time can be used in many ways to incorporate math activities, including the following:

- When children arrive in our classroom each morning, they are asked to answer a question that gathers data about our class members, add to a class graph, or estimate the number of objects in an "estimation jar." Children look forward to these activities each morning, and the activities also serve to give them direction until morning meeting starts.

- At times, we use a sweep hand alarm clock that is set to the time of our next special class (art, gym, or music). When the alarm clock goes off, children look at the hands on the clock and begin to understand the concept of time. Alarm clocks can also be set to go off at every hour on the hour, to teach time to the hour, or they can be set for specific periods of time, such as five minutes, to give children a better concept of time.

- Children in our classroom walk in pairs as they travel to various locations for special classes, recess,

A daily survey builds sight-word vocabulary and provides regular opportunities to meet the data and probability standard.

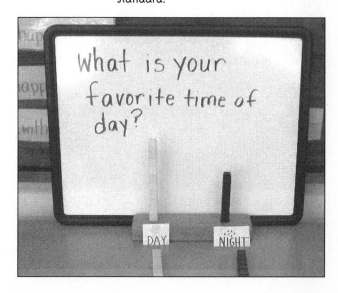

and lunch. The pairs of children can be used to count by twos and for one-to-one correspondence as we make sure everyone has a partner. Children begin to understand the concept of multiples of two when they count off as pairs. Once children line up, we notice the beginning, middle, and end of the line. Not only does this give children an opportunity to name locations and relationships (a geometry skill), but it can also be used as an analogy for story writing, as every story needs a beginning, middle, and end!

Songs, Chants, and Poems

Songs, chants, and poems are an everyday part of a kindergarten classroom. They're a great way to start and end the day, and make wonderful and meaningful teaching tools for phonics lessons during the morning meeting. Combine them with manipulatives to strengthen math skills and concepts. Traditional songs such as "Five Little Pumpkins Sitting on the Gate," "The Farmer in the Dell," "The Twelve Days of Christmas" (which can be changed to The Twelve Days of Winter, Spring, Summer, Fall, or School), and "Five Little Ducks Went Out to Play" support a curriculum that is rich in math connections.

This rhyme teaches number sense.

Snack Time

Our snack is a self-serve option during Choice Time. When children go to the snack center, they follow the day's menu to determine their snack portion. Children eagerly follow the menu, counting out their portion. The menu is made from a series of photos of food with print labeling the food. I laminate these cards so they can be used again and again. Numbers with coinciding shapes to determine the amount are written on small pieces of tagboard and laminated. The numbers and food labels are attached to a larger piece of tagboard with Velcro. Sometimes, the food must be counted by scoops, other times individually. As the year progresses, the snack menus may grow to represent the portions in other ways. For example, instead of having five crackers, a child can have two crackers and three crackers.

Calendar Time

Many math concepts come up during our daily calendar session. The beauty of teaching the calendar every day is that, if well thought out and taught appropriately, it usually addresses most, if not all, of the standards. When children manipulate the calendar each day, they are learning in small increments, but over the course of time, they have amassed large bodies of mathematical knowledge. The calendar encompasses a wide variety of math activities that span the standards.

As part of our calendar session each morning, we keep track of the number of days that we have been in school. When we reach the 100th day, we have a special celebration. Each child creates a collection of 100 objects at home. Their collections become part of a class "One Hundreds Museum." Throughout the day, we celebrate with various 100th Day math activities, such as reading 100 books collectively, making the words "one hundred" out of dough and baking it, and sorting many objects into different groupings to make 100. (For more information on Calendar Time, see Chapter 4.)

A snack menu builds more math practice into every day.

Parents and other classes are invited to see our 100th Day collections for a cost of one hundred dollars per person. (Not to worry, pretend one hundred dollar bills are given out at the door.)

TEACHING MATH AT CHOICE TIME

In addition to the math center, the block center and science center lend themselves well to teaching math concepts. Plans for the block center begin on page 63; the math and science centers are outlined on pages 78–81. Here's a closer look at making math connections at each of these centers.

These boys are experimenting with probability as they construct a marble race game.

MATH CENTER: At the math center, children actively explore materials, making patterns and sorting and classifying. To extend mathematical concepts at the center, try these suggestions:

- Have children practice using nonstandard measurements by measuring with a tower of Unifix cubes.
- As children work with color tiles, counting bears, and other counters, introduce addition and subtraction concepts.
- Stretch patterning skills by asking children to find and describe patterns in the room, and then to recreate them with manipulatives. Use patterning cards to help children make and extend patterns.
- Introduce place value as children explore base ten blocks.
- As children begin to feel more comfortable with formal math, ask them to record their thinking, or share it with an adult who can help them record it.
- When children group and sort materials, ask them to show numbers in other ways. For example, a group of seven objects can be shown as three objects and four objects, or as five and two.
- Have children explore symmetry by creating shapes and patterns with Geoboards.

BLOCK CENTER: At the block center, children can plan and design buildings using patterning, geometry, reasoning, and problem solving. To extend mathematical learning, try these suggestions:

- Invite children to name, build, sort, and compare shapes as they consider different architectural aspects of structures.

Math Talk

As children participate in activities with mathematical connections, ask questions to extend their thinking. For example:

- Can you show me another way?
- How did you arrive at that answer?
- What would happen if...?
- What does this show?
- How could you...?
- How are these the same? How are they different?
- What caused...?
- How do you know...?

This boy is exploring how different materials will work for a marble race.

Math All Around

Although the block, math, and science centers are prime areas for exposure to math concepts, other centers have math value as well. At the art center, children create using patterns, geometric shapes, and symmetry. Brushes and paint pots provide for practice with one-to-one correspondence. When drawing and painting, children consider positions in space, as well as size. At the dramatic play center, children use one-to-one correspondence and beginning number operations as they set the table and serve meals. Fraction concepts come into play as children share materials among the group. Telephone books, paper, and pencils invite explorations with numbers. When the dramatic play center is turned into a store, there are many opportunities for children to use money, problem solving, and counting.

- Use unit blocks to reinforce commonly used fractions, such as one half and one fourth.
- Teach the language of mathematics as children plan and build their structures. For example, discuss relative positions of blocks *(on top of, next to, over, under)*.
- Encourage children to measure their structures using standard and nonstandard measurement.
- Promote communication in mathematics by asking children to record their plans on "blueprint" paper (which can simply be blue paper!).

SCIENCE CENTER: The science center is an ideal environment for making math connections. As children observe animals and plants, they pose questions and gather data, sort and classify, and compare and order objects. When they record their findings in science logs and journals, they get firsthand experience with data analysis and probability. Measurement is also a natural extension of the science area. Try these ideas to extend children's mathematical thinking here:

- Let children compare objects by

Working with water at the science center helps children develop measuring skills and understand conservation of matter.

weighing them on a balance scale.

• Ask children to use different tools to make standard and nonstandard measurements. Have them make estimates based on their measurements.

• Invite children to notice patterns and symmetry in natural items at the science center, such as on a snake, butterfly, or leaves.

• Guide children in creating graphs and representing data using concrete objects or pictures.

• Arrange for guest speakers to give children a new perspective on the use of math in science in daily life.

TEACHING MATH WITH CHILDREN'S LITERATURE

Many children's books make connections to math concepts, some in very obvious ways, others more subtly. Using the language of mathematics while sharing a story supports mathematical thinking. However, it is important that the math concepts flow naturally. Following are mini-lesson starters to use with children's literature.

ACT IT OUT: Math-based books—such as *The Doorbell Rang* by Pat Hutchins (Mulberry Books, 1986), *Five Little Monkeys Jumping on the Bed* by Eileen Christelow (Clarion Books, 1989), *The Very Hungry Caterpillar* by Eric Carle (Putnam, 1983), and *The Grouchy Ladybug* by Eric Carle (HarperCollins, 1977)—are wonderful for dramatizing events and gaining a better understanding of math concepts such as number sense, time, shapes, and patterns.

SIZE ORDER: Discuss characters using math terms, such as smallest, biggest, tallest, and shortest. For example, using *The Seven Silly Eaters* by Mary Ann Hoberman (Harcourt Brace, 1997), children can compare the seven siblings by age (who was born first, next, and so on) and by size.

COUNTING BY THREES: Build a foundation for multiplication skills with fairy tales, which often have magical elements or events that happen in threes. Ask children to count how many magical things happen in a fairy tale and discuss them after sharing the story. Start a display of magical events in fairy tales. Have children draw

More Math-Based Children's Books

More favorite children's books that make strong math connections are:

Fish Eyes: A Book You Can Count On by Lois Ehlert (Harcourt, 1990): Children love the illustrations in this book of brightly colored fish to count.

Moja Means One: Swahili Counting Book by Muriel L. Feelings (Dial Press, 1971): Beautiful charcoal drawings depict the African landscape as children learn to count in English and Swahili.

1 Is One by Tasha Tudor (Simon & Schuster, 1956): A Caldecott Honor winner with rich watercolor illustrations, this book counts to 20 beautifully.

Ten Black Dots by Donald Crews (Greenwillow Books, 1986): Discover what one black dot can make, then two, and so on. Great to use as a writing template!

pictures of the events. Use the growing groups of three for counting activities.

PROBLEMS AND SOLUTIONS: Many books, such as *Sheila Rae, the Brave* by Kevin Henkes (Greenwillow, 1996), feature characters with a problem to solve. Build problem-solving and reasoning skills by inviting children to suggest their own ideas for handling a difficult situation.

MAKING REAL-LIFE CONNECTIONS: Some children's books invite real-life comparisons that use math skills. For example, after sharing Tomie dePaola's *Strega Nona* (Simon & Schuster, 1975), children can calculate how much spaghetti they would need to feed their class. (Of course, cooking the spaghetti and sauce also is loaded with math concepts.)

TEACHING MATH WITH THEMATIC UNITS

Mathematics is made meaningful when it is integrated into the curriculum naturally, such as through thematic units of study that make practical mathematical connections. For instance, a unit on Creepy Crawlies invites children to count an insect's body parts and compare them to those of a spider (which means more counting). As children compare their numbers, they build number sense, looking at the differences between the numbers (which one is bigger, more than, less than, and so on). Of course, the math connections go on and on in such a unit to meet many of the math standards. For example, children can:

- Investigate big numbers as they research how many insects there are.
- Explore size order (which is the biggest insect? the smallest?).
- Describe and extend patterns (a monarch butterfly caterpillar, for example, has a pattern of green, yellow, and black).
- Collect and analyze data (in a class survey, for example, on favorite insects).
- Identify shapes (in insects' body parts).
- Recognize shapes that have symmetry (for example, in a ladybug's wings).
- Sort and classify insects according to traits (life-cycle traits; physical traits such as wings or no wings).

Just one unit like this easily and naturally covers many of the kindergarten math standards. (For more information on teaching with themes, see Chapter 9.)

Keep in Mind...

"...child-centered curriculum is too often interpreted as 'child indulgent,' and a more descriptive term would be 'child sensitive.' The goal of child-centered curriculum is to base curriculum decisions first and foremost on the needs of children and the ways in which children learn."

—from *Reaching Potentials: Appropriate Curriculum and Assessment for Young Children, Volume I,* Sue Bredekamp and Teresa Rosegrant, Editors (National Association for the Education of Young Children, 1992)

Especially for Half-Day Kindergarten

In a half-day kindergarten, math time might be scheduled to run simultaneously with Choice Time, in place of, or added to, other Choice Time activities.

MATH TIME MINI-LESSONS AND ACTIVITIES

Planning for math lessons in the classroom starts by "kid watching" with keen eyes and good listening habits. I want to tailor math activities to fit the needs of each child. I use concepts that children are just beginning to understand as the launching point for mini-lessons. From there, I plan math activities using a "math station" format. I want these activities to excite children about math and to scaffold new strategies and concepts onto their prior knowledge. (See pages 147–156 for more on math station groups and activities.)

Introducing a Mini-Lesson

After singing along to "Number Rock," children settle on the rug and get ready for a math mini-lesson. Often I will use the overhead projector simply because children think it is the neatest thing, and it gets me their undivided attention quite easily. Sometimes the mini-lesson begins with a children's book; after reading it, we discuss it and act out the math lessons it contains.

Mini-lessons are based on NCTM standards and are directly related to at least one of the math stations that I have set up. As I watch children during math time, I begin to plan mini-lessons based on what children are having difficulty with or where they need to extend their learning. This is a time for explicit teaching, a time to use the language of mathematics, and a time to clear up any misunderstandings children may have. Following is a sample mini-lesson.

Using mini-lessons gives a teacher information about a child's thinking and reasoning skills.

Number and Operations Mini-Lesson

To address the Number and Operations standard—specifically, to develop a sense of whole numbers and to connect number words and numerals to the quantities they represent—I share *Counting Our Way to Maine* by Maggie Smith (Orchard Books, 1995). This is a story about a family taking a vacation to Maine. They count as they pack the car for the vacation, as they enjoy their vacation, and again as they prepare to go home. I prepare a prop bag representing the items they count, and make matching number cards. Children match props from the bag to number cards in order to represent the story. For example, the family sees 13 boats on their vacation. A child choosing a toy boat from the bag would select the number card 13 to represent the number of boats the family counted. Extensions of the mini-lesson are endless. Children can show the number of items in different ways, such as by using manipulatives or drawing a picture on the overhead. They can also count backwards to pack the car and return home. Following a math mini-lesson, children move on to math stations, at which they practice the skills and concepts covered.

Setting up Math Stations

A "math station" approach makes it easy to tailor math lessons to the needs of each child. Groupings of two to three students work well. This gives children more opportunities to use the language of math and explain their reasoning to one another. Smaller groupings also give me more control over the dynamic of the group and the type of learning that will take place. For example, I might place two children in a group together who have different strengths so that they can share their understandings with each other. Other times I might place two children in a group who share a need to work on specific skills, allowing me to focus my attention on both children at once.

Math stations are portable and kept in baskets until it is time for math time. For example, a station that requires pattern blocks would be located near the manipulative area. A basket of other materials needed for work at this station would be set next to the pattern blocks. Depending on the number of children in the classroom, I usually set up seven to ten math station activities, all built on a spiral curriculum using the NCTM standards. Children spend from 20 to 30 minutes at a station, depending on the activities and the interests of the children. Following are eight sample stations that represent a variety of develop-

Scheduling Math Time

I schedule formal math time two afternoons per week. Children work in groups at a different math station on both of these days. With eight stations and eight groups of children, I have enough stations to last four weeks (two days of math per week times four weeks equals eight stations). However, I run the same math stations for five weeks, as I include time for children to explore the stations as they wish at the end of the rotation. During this last week, children can revisit favorite activities, making their own math connections.

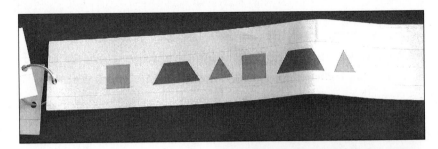

TiP

Extending The Work

During the math station time, my job is to circulate around the room asking questions that extend children's math learning. This is also a time to work with individual children as needed. When children finish their math station work, they are encouraged to use the materials in a different way—for example, after extending a pattern, they may use the blocks to create a new pattern. Or they may use other math materials that are not being used by other groups.

Numbers on the back of puzzle pieces correspond to dots on the backing.

mental levels, and a list of the standards that each supports. Use them as models for your own math station activities.

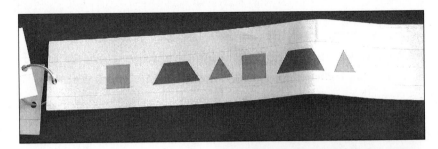

MATH STATION ACTIVITY 1: Pattern Books

Glue pattern block cutouts to sentence strips to show a partial pattern. (You can bind several of these to make a patterning book.) Have children place pattern blocks on the sentence strips to complete the patterns. Children then use pattern blocks to make their own patterns, and represent the patterns by gluing pattern block cutouts to sentence strips.

Extensions: Identify the types of patterns (A–B, A–B–C, and so on). To make new patterns, trace objects in the classroom or cut other shapes from construction paper.

STANDARDS CONNECTIONS

Understanding Patterns: Recognizing, describing, and extending patterns.

Number and Operations: Understanding numbers, counting.

Geometry: Analyzing characteristics and properties of shapes.

Reasoning and Proof: Using logical reasoning to approach a problem.

Communication: Communicating mathematical knowledge through pictures.

MATH STATION ACTIVITY 2: Puzzles

Display several puzzles. Have children work together, using the language of math to assemble the puzzles. For example, children might use the language of problem solving, informally formulating questions and gathering data to complete the puzzle.

Extensions: Using puzzles that come with a cardboard form backing (found at most discount stores), write a number on the back of each puzzle piece. Draw the corresponding number of dots on the cardboard form backing of that puzzle piece. This gives children another opportunity to use counting skills as they work with puzzles. There are many variations on this idea: matching uppercase and lowercase letters, solving addition and subtraction problems, and putting color words and color spots together.

MATH STATION
ACTIVITY 3: Measure the School

This is an activity that can use either nonstandard or standard measurement. Give children copies of the reproducibles on pages 160–163 (The Official Measure the School Book). Have children cut apart the pages and staple to bind. With adult supervision, have children measure the items listed.

Extensions: Ask children to make a drawing to represent the items they measured, from smallest to largest. Have children represent their findings in a graph. For a variation of this activity, ask children to count different items in the school.

Clipboards are fun and useful props for gathering math information.

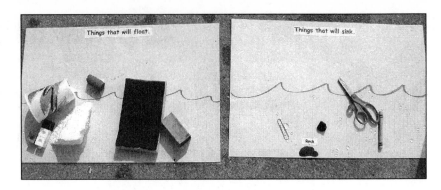

Customizing the Standards for Kindergarten

In *The Young Child and Mathematics* (National Association for the Education of Young Children, 2000), Juanita V. Copley discusses the standards and how to decide where to place the emphasis in kindergarten: "For children in prekindergarten through second grade, NCTM guidance strongly emphasizes numbers and geometry. About half as much emphasis is given to the areas of measurement and data analysis. Algebra receives the least attention, although pattern awareness and understanding, which are fundamental in algebraic thinking, are a strong thread throughout the early childhood standards."

MATH STATION ACTIVITY 4: Float or Sink?

Set up the sensory table or a tub of water with a variety of items and two laminated charts, one labeled "Things That Will Float" with a picture depicting an object floating and one labeled "Things That Will Sink" with a picture of an object sinking. Ask children to test the items and determine if they will float or sink. Have them place the items on the chart to show the outcome of their test.

Extensions: Have children make and document a hypothesis of what will float or sink before beginning this activity. Let them make a real or representational graph to show their results. Count the items in each category on the graph and find the difference between the two.

STANDARDS CONNECTIONS

Data Analysis: Posing questions and gathering data. Sorting and classifying objects according to their properties. Making graphs to demonstrate data.

Algebra: Sorting objects by properties.

Number and Operations: Understanding meanings of operations and how they relate to one another.

Reasoning and Proof: Using reasoning to reach mathematical results.

Communication: Organizing mathematical thinking through communication.

Connections: Applying mathematical concepts outside of mathematics.

MATH STATION ACTIVITY 5: Marble Race

Have children place a one-foot piece of PVC pipe on the ground. (A paper towel tube also works well, as pictured on page 151.) Ask them to roll a marble through the pipe, and to measure how far the marble travels on the floor (using standard or nonstandard measurement, depending on the level of the children). Next, have them take turns trying to make the marble roll further—for example, by holding the pipe in different ways (closer to the floor, further from the floor, and so on).

It's fun to roll a marble through PVC pipe or paper towel rolls, and then measure how far it goes.

Extensions: Have children explain what they think will happen when they hold the pipe at different angles. Ask children to make a graph showing how far the marble rolled when the pipe was held at different angles. (Adapted from *The Young Child and Mathematics* by Juanita V. Copley.)

MATH STATION ACTIVITY 6:
Making Numerals

Provide children with different materials to make numbers—for example, they can shape Wikki Stix and play clay into numbers. They can use sand trays and shaving cream mats to carve out numbers with fingers. They can trace tagboard numbers on sandpaper and cut them out to make their own tactile numbers.

Extensions: Ask children to put the numbers in order. Have children use manipulatives to show the numbers in different ways.

Using materials like Wikki Stix to form numbers appeals to a young child's kinesthetic learning style.

Children take turns ordering and serving, building math skills each time.

MATH STATION ACTIVITY 7: Kindergarten Hamburger Stand

Use felt to make foods associated with a hamburger stand: brown felt for hamburgers, tan felt for buns, light green for lettuce, red for tomatoes, dark green for pickles, and yellow for cheese squares. Supply the station with empty, clean condiment bottles. Cut yellow sponges in French fry-length strips. Collect food containers, bags, and any other appropriate items from fast food restaurants.

Extensions: Have children use a menu to order, circling their choices. (For a reproducible menu, see page 164.) The child serving must count the number of items back to the child ordering. Provide cash registers and pretend money to let children play with counting out money and making change. Variations on this idea: The Sunny Side Up Restaurant, using felt for eggs, bacon, sausage, homefries, and toast; a pancake house with felt pancakes.

Math Sharing Time

After children finish their math stations for the day, we return to the meeting area to discuss what they learned. As children share their reasoning and thinking skills and explain how they problem solved at the math stations, their classmates begin to look at math in different ways.

STANDARDS CONNECTIONS

Number and Operations: Understanding relationships among numbers. Using computing skills.

Algebra: Sorting and classifying.

Geometry: Recognizing and naming shapes.

Data Analysis: Representing data using concrete objects.

Communication: Using the language of mathematics to communicate what is known.

Connections: Making connections between math and daily life.

MATH STATION ACTIVITY 8: Cereal Math

This is an old favorite and makes a fun homework assignment, too. Provide sandwich bags or small cups of colorful cereal pieces and a sorting mat. (See reproducible sorting mat, page 165.) Guide children in coloring the cereal shapes on the sorting mat to match the words, then let them sort the cereal by color.

Extensions: Hot-glue pieces of cereal to tagboard cards. Have children stack the cards to play the following game: They take turns drawing two cards from the pile. They then see how many cereal pieces they have in those colors and use the numbers to make an addition or subtraction problem. Children can record their number sentences on the back of their sorting mats.

More Math Station Starters

In addition to the eight math station activities outlined on pages 148–153, here are a few more activities to meet each of the math standards. Any of these would work well at a math station, or as a whole-class activity.

The Number and Operations Standard

"COUNT THE SCHOOL" MINI-BOOK: Photocopy the reproducibles on pages 166–169 and laminate before binding to make a reuseable book. Ask children to count the items listed in the book and write their findings with a wet-erase pen on the laminated pages.

LUNCH BAG BOOKS: Make books from lunch bags. Draw a group of items (or paste a picture) on each bag. Write the number of objects inside on the bottom flap of each bag. Bind the bags along the left to make a book. Children can count the objects, and then open the flap on the bottom of each bag to reveal the number.

PIGGY BANK MATCH: After reading *A Chair For My Mother* by Vera B. Williams (Greenwillow, 1982), let children count coins into a piggy bank and make up number sentences to go with them.

BLUEBERRY DIVISION: After reading *Blueberries for Sal* by Robert McCloskey (Viking Press, 1948), have children in small groups

Rote and Rational Counting

There is a difference between rote counting and counting rationally. Rote counting involves memorizing numbers and repeating them in a given order. Rational counting is achieved when a child uses one-to-one correspondence, counting in a stable order. When a child rationally counts, it does not matter which item is counted first, just that the last number is the total number of objects counted (the cardinal principle).

divide a pint of blueberries equally between themselves. If real blueberries are not available, spray paint dried beans blue. (Check for allergies before using real blueberries.)

PAPER PLATE MATH: Write numbers on paper plates. Draw or paste pictures on the plates to represent each number. Give each child a plate. Call out different games for children to play with the plates. For example, call out, "Let's Make a Match" to have children try to find someone with the same number. Call out, "Let's Make a Train" to have children put themselves in order from the smallest to the greatest number. Call out, "Let's Add Up" to have children team up to make number sentences with a target sum.

Make socks into puppets by gluing on felt facial features and googly eyes.

The Algebra Standard

PUT THE STORY IN ORDER: Make props children can use to put the events of a story in order. For example, after reading *The Very Hungry Caterpillar* by Eric Carle (Philomel, 1994), children can use a sock-puppet caterpillar to eat through tagboard cutouts of the food from the story—in the same order as in the story.

SOUNDS LIKE A PATTERN: Use musical instruments to make sound patterns and have children repeat the pattern. (Instruments can be as simple as pencils tapping on a desk.)

HAVE A BALL WITH MATH: Use bouncing balls to make different patterns. Let children bounce their own balls to extend the pattern.

LET'S LINE UP: Have children line up by certain characteristics—for example, the type of shoes they're wearing ("Everyone wearing Velcro sneakers may line up," "Everyone wearing buckle shoes may line up," and so on) or a color they aren't wearing ("Everyone not wearing blue today may line up," "Everyone not wearing yellow may line up," and so on).

The Geometry Standard

MIRROR MATH: Use tangram patterning cards to make patterns. Let children hold up small mirrors to show symmetry.

UNDER, ABOVE, NEXT TO: After reading a story, use flannelboard pieces to retell it. Have children place the characters and objects on the board as they describe relative positions in space (next to, under, above, and so on).

TRACE AND MATCH: Make tagboard tracings of classroom objects, such as paper clips, pencils, rubber bands, and scissors. Let children find the real objects in the classroom and match them to the tracings.

The Measurement Standard

SENSORY TABLE SCOOPING: At the sensory table, have children measure rice, beans, or other small objects. Have them record how many scoops it takes to fill specific containers.

WATCH US GROW: Measure each child's height once a month. Compare growth from one month to the next. Keep a record for children to have as a keepsake at the end of the year.

SHAPE FILL-INS: Ask children to find the area of large shape cutouts by filling in the shape with Unifix cubes.

TALLEST TO SHORTEST: Use gift wrap, paper towel, and bathroom tissue rolls to make graduated cylinders. Have children put them in order from shortest to tallest or tallest to shortest.

Children build with blocks and use cutouts of the shapes to replicate the structure.

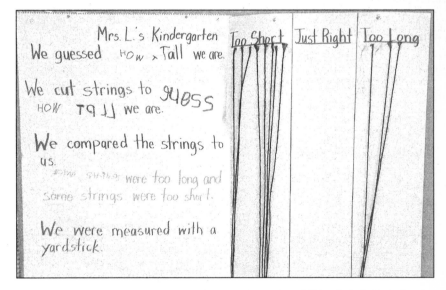

Measuring children's height each month involves estimating, measuring, comparing, and calculating.

The Data Analysis Standard

GREAT GRAPHS: Create a standard form for at-home surveys, in which children interview family members about favorite color, food, time of day, and so on. Compile and graph findings.

SPIDER OR INSECT? At the end of an insect unit, have children use clay to create either an insect or a spider, not revealing their choice to

TiP

Graphing Ideas

Following are questions to use for family surveys. (They work for class surveys, too.) Invite children to suggest others.

• What is your favorite movie?

• Do you like pizza?

• What month is your birthday in?

• Do you like to read?

• What is your favorite book?

• Have you ever traveled to ___?

• Do you have a brother? A sister?

• If you could take a vacation, where would you go?

classmates. Have classmates then decide which each creation is—either spider or insect, based on the attributes.

TAKE A VOTE: Have children add their "vote" to a graph. Set up graphs to answer questions such as "Would you choose to be something scary or not scary for Halloween?" or "Do you like mornings or afternoons better?"

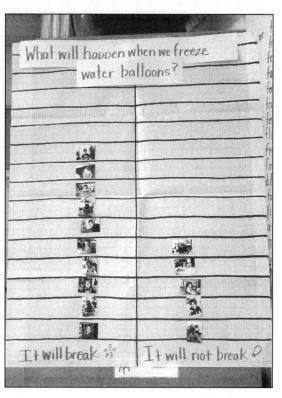

Children's photos make great graph markers!

SORT IT OUT: Using an assortment of commercial counters, such as bears or bugs, have children sort them by attribute. Cupcake tins make fun sorting containers.

ASSESSMENT STRATEGIES FOR MATH

The only real reason assessments should be used is to support students in their learning. When we carefully listen to and observe children as they grapple with problems and discuss their reasoning, we gain true insights into what children know and where they need to go next with their learning. With this in mind, following are several strategies for assessing students' learning in math.

CHECKLISTS: Genuine learning and discovery cannot be pigeonholed into checklists; however, you may find them helpful for a piece of the assessment process.

> **January 15**
> Danny is making groupings of two and counting by twos with teddy bear counters.

> **October 5**
> Mia is extending patterns using pattern blocks and naming colors and shapes.

ANECDOTAL RECORDS: During observations of children, and conversations with them, I document insights into their learning as anecdotal records, often writing remarks on sticky notes. (See page 193.) I include these comments as part of a narrative for each child's progress report.

LESSON EVALUATIONS: An assessment piece that is sometimes forgotten in the classroom is the assessment we do on our own teaching practices. When lessons are planned and carried out, we need to continually evaluate the effectiveness of our teaching. When we can step back and take a long look with a clear mind, it helps to point us in the next direction that our teaching needs to take. That direction should always be the same direction the children are going.

MATH AND THE HOME-SCHOOL CONNECTION

Many parents understand the importance of reading to their children and try to do so on a regular basis. The awareness about how reading to children affects their academic growth is widespread. The importance of everyday math and the benefits of using it with children are not as well known. To encourage families to make math connections like these, share the following ideas.

CALENDAR MATH: Every single day there is an opportunity for math as parents and children look at the calendar together and count how many days until Grandma visits, or when the next family vacation will be. Send home a calendar each month. Ask families to complete it together, recording special events, appointments, holidays, and so on. Have them use it to count the days!

IN THE NEWS: If you send home a weekly newsletter, you might include a regular "Family Math" corner in which you offer a few

Meeting More Standards

In addition to the content standards specifically addressed by the activities on pages 153–156, the NCTM standards include five process standards: Problem Solving, Reasoning and Proof, Communication, Connections, and Representation. These are mathematical processes that are found within each of the five content standards. Children use these processes when they use math in daily activities. For example, when children participate in the sensory-table scooping activity, they are also making connections between the real world and mathematics, representing their data on paper, and using mathematical reasoning as they investigate how many scoops will fill each container. Keep connections like these in mind as you note the ways in which various math activities support the standards.

Internet Resources

In addition to the books listed in the Teacher Resources on page 159, the following Web sites provide useful information and activities for a kindergarten math program:

Discovery School (discoveryschool.com/schrockguide): There are several math-teaching links at this site, including lesson plans and hands-on activities.

Dr. Jean (drjean.org): This site is geared for early childhood, and includes easily made math games and activities for kindergartners.

National Council of Teachers of Mathematics (nctm.org): This comprehensive Web site includes a complete set of the standards along with activities to support them.

Oriental Trading Co. (orientaltrading.com): A great place to find small items to count and sort, or specialty items to make games with.

suggestions for making math connections—for example, counting the recyclables to return, reading prices at the grocery store, determining the amount of food needed for portions at dinner time, following a recipe, checking the time of a favorite TV show, looking up a phone number, counting out lunch money, and checking a calendar for upcoming events.

MONTHLY HOMEWORK: At the beginning of each month, send home eight to twelve activities for children to work on with someone in their family (for that month). These activities might include watching parents balance the checkbook, looking at numbers in a grocery store, or discovering a math connection in a children's book. These activities serve two purposes: to better acquaint children with math concepts, and to help parents think about different math activities they can use in daily life with their children.

INTERACTIVE MINI-BOOKS: Laminated interactive mini-books make special rotating homework assignments. Children record their answers as necessary using a wet-erase pen, which can be wiped off to get the book ready for the next child. There are two samples included in this book. "Math at My House" (see pages 170–173) invites children and their families to count doors, pets, clocks, and so on. To make the "Keeper of the Keys" book, photocopy page 174 and cut apart the two pages. Place them in order (cover, letter), and then add blank pages. On each blank page, write a number and the word *key(s)*: "1 key," "2 keys," "3 keys," and so on. For a challenge, add pages that introduce addition: 1 key + 1 key, 1 key + 2 keys, and so on. Attach a set of old keys to the mini-book. Children will count out the keys to match each page.

Math at My House

Name Dylan

TEACHER RESOURCES

Aims Education Foundation (888-SEE-AIMS; aimsedu.org): AIMS is well known for combining problem-solving skills with math and science skills. In addition to targeting all of these skills, the activities hold a lot of appeal for young children. Lots of reproducibles!

Cereal Math by Karol L. Yeatts (Scholastic, 2000): This activity book features lots of reproducibles and activities for using cereal in math lessons, and addresses all of the NCTM standards.

Fresh & Fun: 100th Day of School by Jacqueline Clarke (Scholastic, 2001): This creative collection of ideas from teachers across the country includes games, calendar activities, pocket chart poems, songs, book links, and more for making your 100th day celebration extra special. More than a dozen other titles in the Fresh & Fun series each include a section on math. All books include a big, colorful poster with teaching activities.

Irresistible 1, 2, 3s by Joan Novelli (Scholastic Professional Books, 1999): Introduce numbers and teach counting with the games, art projects, learning center ideas, poems, and manipulatives in this creative resource.

Mathematics Their Way by Mary Baratta-Lorton (Pearson Learning, 1994): This program is a great resource for hands-on games and activities.

Macmillan Early Skills Manipulatives (Newbridge Educational Publishers, 1993): This company sells ready-made manipulative kits, including the manipulatives, games, and reproducibles for different math skills.

Miquon Math Lab Series by Lore Rasmussen (Key Curriculum Press, 1978): This hands-on math program is good for upper-level kindergarten through third grade.

Mother Goose Math by Deborah Schecter (Scholastic Professional Books, 2003): This engaging resource uses favorite nursery rhymes to make early math skills and concepts come alive for young learners. Includes hands-on games, activities, and manipulatives that foster learning. Linked to the NCTM standards.

The Young Child and Mathematics by Juanita V. Copley (National Association for the Education of Young Children, 2000): This practical math book is organized by the NCTM standards and has developmentally appropriate sample lessons and activities for each standard.

The Official Measure the School Book

By _____

A school lunch tray

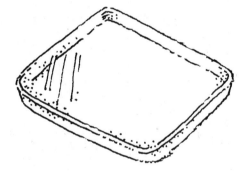

is this long:

_____

The New Kindergarten: Teaching Reading, Writing & More • Scholastic Professional Books

The principal's desk

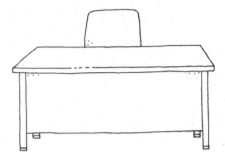

is this long:

_____

3

- -

The secretary's stapler

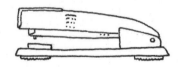

is this long:

_____

4

Our favorite book

in the library is this long:

_____

5

The music teacher's piano

is this long:

_____

6

The New Kindergarten: Teaching Reading, Writing & More • Scholastic Professional Book

The biggest ball

in the gym
has a circumference of:

_____

7

The _____

in the _____

_____:

_____

8

Name _____ Date _____

Hamburger Stand Menu

bun	o	1	2	3
meat	o	1	2	3
cheese	o	1	2	3
lettuce	o	1	2	3
tomato	o	1	2	3
pickle	o	1	2	3
total	—	—	—	—

The New Kindergarten: Teaching Reading, Writing & More • Scholastic Professional Books

Cereal Math
Sorting Mat

red ◎

blue ◎

yellow ◎

green ◎

purple ◎

orange ◎

The Official
Count the School
Book

Counters:

_____

_____

How many people

in the office?

_____

The New Kindergarten: Teaching Reading, Writing & More • Scholastic Professional Books

How many chalkboards

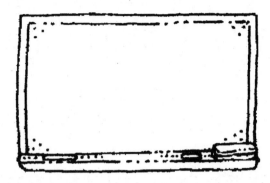

in the classroom?

_____

How many school buses

in the parking lot?

_____

How many trash cans

in the lunchroom?

_____

5

How many chairs

in the classroom?

_____

6

The New Kindergarten: Teaching Reading, Writing & More • Scholastic Professional Books

How many _____

in the _____?

_____

7

How many _____

in the _____?

_____

8

Math at My House

Name _____

Dear Families,

This is an interactive book. Please have your child count the specified items in your home. Your child can use the special pen (included in this package) to write in the book. Have fun!

Sincerely,

_____

How many doors

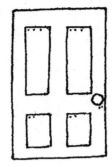

in your house?

_____

How many pets

in your house?

_____

How many clocks

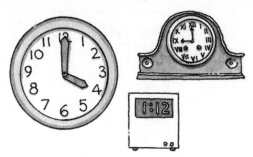

in your house?

_____

5

How many people

in your house?

_____

6

The New Kindergarten: Teaching Reading, Writing & More • Scholastic Professional Books

How many windows

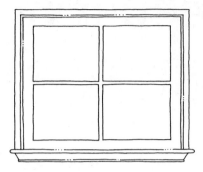

in your house?

_____

How many _____

in your house?

_____

Keeper of The Keys

Name _____

1

Dear Families,

This is an interactive book. Please have your child put the specified number of keys on each page. Invite your child to count the keys. Have fun!

Sincerely,

_____

2

The New Kindergarten: Teaching Reading, Writing & More • Scholastic Professional Books

THE KINDER GARDEN

CHAPTER 9

Teaching With Themes

In the dramatic play area, four children are working diligently, digging up potting soil from the sensory table and planting seeds and small plant shoots. They are conducting experiments to see what grows and what doesn't. Meanwhile, two children are checking their baggie gardens in the science center and recording observations. As the seeds begin to sprout, the children begin to form hypotheses about which items are living and which are nonliving.

Several children are writing in their science journals about the terrariums they've been keeping, and others are poring over books about living things in the reading center. A small group of children are gathered with me planting seeds in an aquarium. The seeds are planted close to the glass sides, and the children hope they will be able to see the root systems as the plants grow.

All of these children are actively engaged in a Living Things thematic unit. Young children learn best by making connections between disciplines, making kindergarten a natural environment for thematic teaching. This chapter begins with important guidelines for teaching with themes and continues with tips for choosing topics, planning a unit, gathering materials, and assessing student learning. A week-by-week unit on friendship shows how to implement thematic teaching to develop skills and concepts across the curriculum in a meaningful context.

WHY TEACH WITH THEMES?

Children learn best when skills and concepts are taught and used in a meaningful context. Naturally, in the world around us, skills and concepts are used in an integrated fashion, and it only makes sense for children to learn to use these skills in the same way. When children are inspired with a reason to learn, they are more willing to seek out answers to their questions. Other reasons to teach with themes include the following:

- When new skills and concepts are introduced to children in a meaningful way, children tend to be more interested in the topic of study.
- Integrated learning lets children learn disciplines as people naturally do in the real world, as they relate to each other. For example, a unit on community connects social studies concepts with reading and writing skills, as children read about communities and write letters to community members.

Especially for Half-Day Kindergarten

When planning a thematic unit for half-day kindergarten, the activities may have to be stretched over a longer period of time. Be especially careful to select only those activities that seem most important, considering your classroom's individual needs.

- Integrated learning helps to ease transitions in young children's days. Instead of chopping the day into literacy, math, social studies, and science segments, all of the disciplines can be taught together while studying a theme. Integrated learning helps children learn to chunk information into groups that can be more easily understood.

A Living Things theme invites children to predict what grows and what doesn't.

GUIDELINES FOR GETTING STARTED

Most of us teaching young children are already using thematic teaching or integrated learning in some way. It's the natural way for young children to learn. In planning an integrated unit, it helps to remember the following guidelines:

- **The thematic unit promotes purposeful learning.** The most important criterion for choosing a thematic unit is whether or not it's meaningful for children. Many themes have cute ideas and adorable projects, and may be very tempting to use. However, as keepers of the curriculum, we must honor children while making sure that a thematic unit substantially contributes to the required curriculum.

- **The thematic unit is rich in content.** The thematic unit of study should lend itself well to many disciplines of the curriculum, helping children to make connections between their frame of reference and the world. If a unit is mostly science based, will there be sufficient math, literacy, and social studies activities to warrant teaching the unit for a significant period of time?

- **The thematic unit takes into consideration knowledge of child development and values individual differences.** When planning a thematic unit of study, learning is guided by the teacher's knowledge of child development. For example, activities within a thematic unit that require a lot of writing may not be developmentally appropriate for most kindergartners. However, taking into account individual differences in children, there are some five- and six-year-olds who are fully capable of writing long passages, and are eager to do so.

- **The thematic unit is rich in language experiences and social interactions.** Thematic units that encourage social interactions and cultivate language-rich experiences are the most beneficial for young

Keep in Mind...

"Although it is clear that topics of interest to the children should be the main focus of a project, it is also important to note that not all interests of the children are equally worthy of the kind of time and effort involved in good project work."

—from *Young Investigators: The Project Approach in the Early Years* by Judy Harris Helm and Lilian Katz (Teachers College Press, 2001)

children. Young children learn within a social context; as they read, write, listen, and speak with one another, they begin to make connections about what they are learning and how it relates to their world. Topics that encourage problem solving and discussion provide a strong language base for children.

TIPS FOR CHOOSING TOPICS

Ideas for thematic units of study can be found in many places. I tend to use the children in my classroom as a springboard for ideas and the kindergarten curriculum guides as a road map. Following are more tips to consider:

- **Keep children in mind when choosing topics.** Children have many interests, and much of what they are interested in makes for worthwhile study. There are many ways to include children in choosing thematic topics. Some teachers choose a topic and ask children to help decide which direction to take it. Other teachers let children choose the entire topic of study. Sometimes a unit evolves from an object that a child brings in that catches the attention of the class. Other times, children begin to show an interest in an activity in the classroom, which leads to a more in-depth study of a topic.

- **Coordinate with district curriculum guides.** Many themes are born out of necessity for teaching district curriculum standards. When I embark on a theme that is based on our district's curriculum frameworks, I try to find areas of the curriculum that seem to have natural links to one another. From there, I build the theme around ideas and activities that give children many opportunities to explore the topic. For example, a unit on living things is based on our district's science curriculum, but within that topic are many opportunities for children to read and write far beyond the area of science.

- **Look ahead to upcoming school events.** Many schools plan whole-grade or school-wide events. Often, these events are "extras" and seem to have no connection to the kindergarten curriculum. One way to make these events more meaningful is to make the event the culminating activity for a thematic unit. For example, our kindergarten classes traditionally visit the fire station and hospital. I've woven these trips into the kindergarten curriculum by including them in a thematic unit on communities. Another way to weave special events into the curriculum is to use the activity itself as a

Family Resources

As I plan for thematic units, I look to families as resources. They may have books, videos, collections, or magazines relating to a topic of study. Many families have taken vacations that lead them to places and things that might be relevant.

starting point for a unit. Let children's questions about the event guide the direction of the unit.

- **Connect curriculum with favorite authors.** Sometimes themes are created around a group of books, or an author study in which several books by the same author are read. Author studies can easily go beyond reading and writing. For example, when I do an author study about Tomie dePaola, I can easily bring in other curriculum areas because his books are so diverse. Children locate where Tomie lives on a map and we bring in geography. When we read *Strega Nona,* we take a trip to the local pasta shop and learn how to make pasta, connecting math with reading recipes, number sense, measurement, and more. The children always write to Tomie (promoting great literacy skills) and Tomie *always* writes back! Receiving mail from a real author is a wonderful incentive for children!

- **Consider seasonal themes.** The time of year can generate a great list of topics for thematic units. For example, children are naturally interested in pumpkins and leaves during the autumn months. Snow and cold weather (if you live in the colder climates) intrigue children in winter. Spring is a great time to begin a study of living things.

GATHERING MATERIALS

Planning for a theme often starts long before the theme is taught. While I'm on family trips in the summer, visiting some obscure store or place or rummaging through things at a flea market, the wheels in my head are turning as I look for items to use in thematic units. I also collect brochures from every rest stop and travel center I stop at, and file them by state so they're easy to find when geographical areas of interest come up.

Plastic tubs also work well for storing materials by theme.

After collecting so many items for thematic units, it's important to find a way to store the items for easy access. I use this simple approach:

- I collect the copy paper boxes with nice lids that the school paper comes in. I label each box with a theme topic and sort materials accordingly.

- I keep a three-ring binder in each box for storing papers, which I organize by subject area—for example, math activities, literacy lessons, community-building ideas, and art projects.

PLANNING THE UNIT

Many teachers use webbing to make a unit plan. To use this approach, I write the topic at the center of the page and record ideas for areas of study around the outer area of the page, connecting them by lines to the topic. From the web, I glean two or three big concepts or guiding questions that I feel are the crux of the unit. What is the real purpose for this unit? What do I want children to take away from this unit? What is most important to their learning?

After I've brainstormed ideas on a web, I begin to outline the unit by weeks. (See Weekly Planner, page 196.) I generally plan on about four weeks per unit. For each week, I list questions I would like children to consider and big concepts that I hope students will uncover during the study.

Using the weekly outlines, I begin to think of activities and projects for individual and small-group work. I label planning pages for each area of the curriculum, and record projects and activities on them. This makes it easy to develop a well-rounded unit that connects math, literacy, science, and so on. These planning pages also make it easy to document the ways in which the unit meets the curriculum standards. I add a planning page for possible field trips, guest speakers, and volunteers, as well as for a unit celebration, which allows children to revisit what they've learned and share it with others in some way, such as through a skit.

This initial planning takes about two to three hours, but it results in plans for a month. I never use the exact set of plans twice, because each class and child is different. But many of the activities and projects can be modified or serve as a springboard for something new.

CREATING A THEME ENVIRONMENT

We often turn the entire classroom into an environment that reflects what we are studying. Children might turn the classroom door into a book for an author study. We hang streamers and ribbon and ocean creatures from the ceiling for an Oceans unit. During

The shower curtain with ocean creatures all over it cost less than a dollar at a close-out store, and it makes a great backdrop for an Oceans unit.

a Rain Forest unit, we added palm trees (made by children) and rain forest animals to the classroom. Children really get excited about this, and look forward to adding to the environment each day.

Each center in the classroom will reflect the unit of study. For example, during a unit on oceans, the dramatic play center might become a boat in a harbor and the science center might feature an aquarium. For a unit on living things, the art center might include leaves, branches, and other items from outdoors for children to paint or collage with.

A READY-TO-USE THEMATIC FRIENDSHIP UNIT

The sample unit that follows is organized by weeks, with goals, activities, and book suggestions for each. Though most units last four weeks, this plan includes activities for five to six weeks. Use the plan as a guide for a unit that meets the needs of your classroom. The unit focuses on community-building activities, making it perfect as a beginning-of-the-year unit.

The environment for this unit will be created by children as they begin to take ownership of the classroom and settle in for the school year. By the end of the unit, the classroom will be alive with projects the children have created during the unit. The bulletin boards and walls will be filled with testaments to our budding friendships in the classroom.

Week 1: Helping children feel secure by establishing routines.
This is the first week of school in my classroom, and I concentrate on helping children feel comfortable, as well as trying to ease any separation anxiety they may have.

Activities for Week 1
STRESS BUSTERS: Plan stress-relieving activities, such as creating with play dough, coloring, building, and looking at books.

OLD FAVORITES: I like to find out what types of activities the children have done in preschool and do some similar activities during this week to make them feel more comfortable. There are some predictable favorites, including painting (especially with different materials, like using a marble dipped in paint to roll across the paper), using tracers to draw pictures, and playing familiar games like "Simon Says."

Alphabet Skills

When I plan a thematic unit of study, I target letters that will naturally work with the unit. For example, for this Friendship unit, the letter *f* is a natural, as are the letters *k* for *kindness* and *t* for *teamwork*.

Week 1
Sing-Alongs

There are all sorts of songs to support a unit on friendship. A few of my favorites are:

"Good Morning" (*We All Live Together, Volume 2* by Greg and Steve; Youngheart, 800-444-4287)

"I Like You, There's No Doubt About It" (*Dr. Jean Sings Silly Songs* by Dr. Jean Feldman; Progressive Music; Crystal Springs Books; 800-321-0401)

"Together Tomorrow" (*Family Tree* by Tom Chapin; Sundance Music; 914-674-0247)

PUZZLE PROJECT: Before school starts, I ask each child or family to decorate a piece of a puzzle that we put together as a class. (See page 21.) During this week, we begin to assemble the puzzle. Some years the words to a community-building song (such as "Make New

JUST-RIGHT READ ALOUDS

Because many children feel separation anxiety when they come to kindergarten, I like to read books that address this issue and let them know how much their families love them, even though they are not with them all the time. Some of my favorites are:

Annabelle Swift, Kindergartner by Amy Schwartz (Orchard Books, 1991): When Annabelle is getting ready to go to kindergarten, her older sister, Lucy, teaches her everything she needs to know—or so Annabelle thinks. This hilarious story is a great start-the-year icebreaker.

Guess How Much I Love You by Sam McBratney (Candlewick Press, 1996): Big Nutbrown Hare and Little Nutbrown Hare try to show each other how much they love each other in this heartwarming book.

Hooray for Diffendoofer Day! by Dr. Seuss, Jack Prelutsky, and Lane Smith (Knopf, 1998): This tale, told in the traditional Seuss rhyming style, celebrates school and learning.

The Kissing Hand by Audrey Penn (Child Welfare League of America, 1993): Chester Raccoon is nervous about starting school. His mother gives him a kiss to save in the palm of his hand.

Mama, Do You Love Me? by Barbara M. Joosse (Chronicle Books, 1998): Set in Inuit territory, a little girl questions her mother's love for her, wondering if her mother would still love her if she got into mischief.

The Night Before Kindergarten by Natasha Wing (Grosset and Dunlap, 2001): Told in the style of *The Night Before Christmas,* this book depicts kindergarten students and their families getting ready for the first day of kindergarten. A wonderful surprise ending thrills kindergartners!

Friends") appear on the puzzle. When the puzzle is complete, we sing the song together.

PICTURE YOURSELF: During the first week of school, I invite children to draw a picture of themselves and to write any words they feel like writing. I date these and save them as baseline writing samples.

KINDERGARTEN DREAMS: As an interactive writing activity, children work together to come up with what they hope will happen in kindergarten. I ask them to think about all of the things they have been wondering about kindergarten as well.

MAKE NEW FRIENDS: Make a class set of children's photos (black and white photocopies are fine). Write each child's name beneath his or her photo. Use O-rings to bind a complete set of photos for each child to take home. Children will enjoy sharing pictures of their classmates with their families, and can begin matching names with faces.

Week 2 Sing-Alongs

As children continue learning songs from the previous week, introduce some new music. Songs that fit well with the activities in Week 2 are:

"So Nice to See You Again" (*Loose Tooth* by Eric Sundberg; Crystal Springs Books; 800-321-0401)

"What A Day It Is" (*Jumping on the Bed* by Eric Sundberg; Crystal Springs Books; 800-321-0401)

Week 2: Making children feel comfortable in the classroom.

During the second week of school, I continue to spend a lot of time introducing materials to children and modeling appropriate behavior in the classroom. I want children to become very familiar with the classroom; the more familiar they are with their surroundings, the more comfortable they will become. This in turn fosters the friendships that will strengthen our class community.

Activities for Week 2

PLANT A GARDEN OF FRIENDS: Children help decorate the bulletin boards in the classroom this week, including one called "Plant a Garden of Friends." Children each make a construction-paper flower and glue a photo or picture of themselves in the middle. For another addition to the bulletin board, children dip the palm of their hand in paint, make a hand print, and cut around it (after the paint is dry). They

Feeling comfortable in the classroom helps create a sense of community.

attach the hand print to the end of a construction-paper stem and add it to the display. During this week and throughout the unit, scribe for children as they tell you positive things about their classmates. Attach these words to a flower shape and add to the display.

CLASS BANNER: Let children agree on a class motto, and make a class banner. Hang it outside the classroom for the remainder of the year.

BIG KIDS IN THE BUILDING! Team up with a teacher of older children for a reading and writing buddies program. Plan a short visit this week with this class. Hold off on actually having the two classes work together; just give them time to get to know each other. Kindergartners love to know some "big kids" in the building!

TOUR THE SCHOOL: Take a tour of the school and introduce children to everyone they will normally come in contact with. Invite the cafeteria staff to meet children and tell them something about their work. Children will feel more comfortable seeing a recognizable face in the sometimes worrisome lunchroom.

NAME TAG NECKLACES: Have children make name tag necklaces to wear to special classes, such as music, art, and physical education. They can trace fun shapes to make the necklaces and go all out with the decorations. Another variation: Supply each child with a plain white T-shirt. Let children decorate their shirts with fabric paint. Write their name and the class name in big letters on the shirt. Children can wear these when they go outside the classroom (to special classes, lunch, and so on) so that everyone will get to know them.

JUST-RIGHT READ ALOUDS

This week, try choosing books that celebrate the differences in people, and in the students in your classroom.

The Berenstain Bears and Too Much Teasing by Stan and Jan Berenstain (Random House, 1995): Brother Bear loves to tease, until the tables are turned. In the end he sees how hurtful teasing can be.

The Butter Battle Book by Dr. Seuss (Random House, 1987): In classic Dr. Seuss style, this book explains the difference between the Zooks and the Yooks—and teaches tolerance in the process.

Emily by Michael Bedard (Doubleday, 1992): A little girl grows up across the street from Emily Dickinson. Although Emily acts very differently than most people (she was a recluse), she has gifts and talents to offer.

Leo the Late Bloomer by Robert Kraus (HarperCollins Juvenile Books, 1987): Leo isn't reading, writing, or speaking. His father is concerned, but his mother isn't. Leo does all of these things in his own good time.

COMFORTABLE CONNECTIONS: Set up pen pals with a relative or friend of each child. Children can exchange letters with the pen pal all year. This creates a comfortable connection for children at school. Later in the year, use writing buddies to help children write letters. Hint: Ask parents to address and stamp envelopes for children to mail their letters.

WHAT MAKES ME COMFORTABLE? Share *Ira Sleeps Over* by Bernard Waber (Houghton Mifflin, 1987). Discuss what makes each of us comfortable. Is it a teddy bear or stuffed animal? Knowing your parents are near? Talk about ways in which children can feel comfortable at school. Follow up with an interactive writing exercise on the topic.

Week 3: Reinforcing The Golden Rule: Treat others as you wish to be treated.

During the third week of school, we begin to focus on respecting others and establishing some guidelines for making our classroom operate. I introduce The Golden Rule on the first day of school and it is discussed throughout the first two weeks, but during this week we begin to focus on others' feelings.

Activities for Week 3

WE CAN HELP: After sharing *Miss Rumphius* by Barbara Cooney (Viking Press, 1982), ask children what they think they could do to make the world a better place. Record each child's response on a sheet of paper. Have children illustrate their sentences. Put the pages together to make a book titled "We Can Help the World." Bring children together in a circle. Pass around the book and let children share their pages with the class.

THE GOLDEN RULE: On a sheet of paper for each child, use glue to write "The Golden Rule." (See page 19.) Let children cover it with glitter and take it home.

FRIENDSHIP BOOKS: Together with children, make a class list of the ways children should treat one another. Write each suggestion on a half sheet of paper and photocopy a set for each child. Let children illustrate the pages and bind them to make a book. Children can take their books home to revisit the ideas with families.

Week 3 Sing-Alongs

As children continue learning songs from the previous week, introduce some new music. Songs that fit well with the activities in Week 3 are:

"I'll Be Around" (*Old Friends, New Friends* by Eric Sundberg; Crystal Springs Books; 800-321-0401)

"Patalina Matalina" (*Dr. Jean and Friends* by Dr. Jean Feldman; Crystal Springs Books; 800-321-0401)

FRIENDLY FISH: After sharing *The Rainbow Fish* by Marcus Pfister (North-South Books, 1992), give each child a foil candy wrapper. (You might want to let children eat the candy first.) Give each child a template of a fish to trace and cut out. On the template, have children write a way they could be friendly to others, like the Rainbow Fish was. Then invite children to glue the colorful candy wrapper "scale" onto their fish. Compile students' fish into a class book about friendship. As a variation, cut out an extra-large fish template. Have children take turns gluing their scales on the large fish as they share a way to be friendly. Record students' ideas on the fish next to their scales.

LITTLE RED HEN'S FRIENDS: Share the story *The Little Red Hen* by Paul Galdone (Houghton Miffflin, 1985), and then discuss how Little Red Hen's friends treated her throughout the book. Act out the story. Use interactive writing to retell the story of the friends, using The Golden Rule as a guide.

JUST-RIGHT READ ALOUDS

This week is a good time to share literature in which characters are presented making good choices, and maybe some poor choices with a lesson. These types of books make great catalysts for discussion on good choices. Books that fit this description follow.

The Children's Book of Virtues by William J. Bennett (Simon & Schuster, 1995): This book uses classic children's literature to teach impressive virtues. The book is divided into categories of courage, responsibility, compassion, and honesty.

Pooh Just Be Nice...and Let Everyone Play by Leslie McGuire (Golden Books, 1997): One of a series of friendship books, this book has Pooh and his friends learning lessons about including everyone.

Strega Nona by Tomie dePaola (Simon & Schuster, 1975): One of my all time favorites! Big Anthony learns a hard lesson about following directions and responsibility while keeping watch over Strega Nona's house.

Swimmy by Leo Lionni (Knopf, 1992): A school of small fish and Swimmy band together to stay safe from the larger fish. A great book about the power of teamwork!

We Share Everything! by Robert N. Munsch (Cartwheel Books, 1999): In the traditional Munsch style, this book will have kids in stitches when two children share *everything* on the first day of kindergarten!

WE'RE ALL HELPERS: Make a class list of the ways children can help others in their school, community, and world. Keep the list and try to work on some of those things throughout the school year.

HAVE A HEART: Make lots of small construction-paper hearts. Keep a basket of these hearts handy. Whenever children "catch" another person being friendly, they can go to the basket and give that person a heart.

Week 4: Helping children make new school friends.

After the first three weeks of school, children have begun to settle into the classroom routine and it's time to work on friendships. During this week, we spend a lot of time enjoying and getting to know each other.

Activities for Week 4

FRIENDLY CONCENTRATION: One of the first steps to literacy for children is reading their names. It makes sense for children to learn all of the names in the classroom and begin to recognize them. Not only is this a nice way to familiarize students with each other, but it also makes an effective literacy tool. Make a concentration game to facilitate this. Photocopy children's pictures and glue them to index cards (one photo per card). Write each child's name on another index card (one name per card). Mix up the cards and place them facedown for a literacy-building game of concentration!

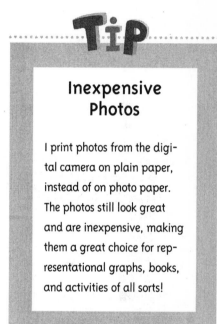

Tip

Inexpensive Photos

I print photos from the digital camera on plain paper, instead of on photo paper. The photos still look great and are inexpensive, making them a great choice for representational graphs, books, and activities of all sorts!

IT'S OUR PHONE BOOK: Remove the front cover of an old phone book. Use it for the cover of a class phone book. To make the book, have children each make a page that includes their photo, name, and phone number on it. (Get parents' permission to use phone numbers.) Variation: Using the copy machine, reduce the pages to make small books for every child to take home. Use this activity as a good baseline assessment of number recognition. This is also a nice activity to use at the end of the school year so children can keep in touch with each other.

GUESS WHO! Give each child a copy of the reproducible on page 197. Have children complete the form and cut along the dashed lines at the bottom to make a flap. Help children glue a sheet of white paper behind this form (placing glue at the edges only and leaving the flap intact). Ask children to

Name _Sarah_ Date _9/8_

Guess Who!

I like to _Play out side_ .

My favorite food is _spagety with grlickbrad_

My favorite color is _yelow_ .

I have _0_ brothers and _1_ sisters.

My eyes are _browh_ .

My hair is _brown_ .

My favorite thing to do is _read_ .

Can you guess who I am?

Week 4
Sing-Alongs

Continue singing songs from previous weeks and introduce a few new ones, for example:

"All I Really Need" (from *Baby Beluga* by Raffi; Troubadour Records, 1977)

"John Jacob Jingleheimer Schmidt" (traditional)

"Puff the Magic Dragon" (traditional)

The Cookie Jar chant is a wonderful way to help children learn to spell each others' names.

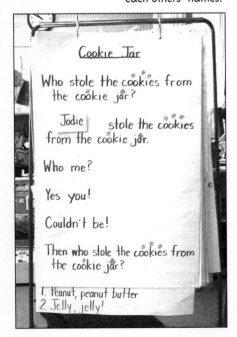

draw or paste a picture of themselves and write their names under the flap. Display and let children try to guess who is behind each flap.

WHAT AM I WEARING? After sharing *Mary Wore Her Red Dress and Henry Wore His Green Sneakers* adapted and illustrated by Merle Peek (Houghton Mifflin, 1988), make a class Big Book in the same format. Children each make a page with their name and what they are wearing, and then illustrate it. Add the book to the classroom library.

LETTER COUNT: Ask children to count the letters in their name. Graph the data, and then use questions to guide a discussion—for example, "How many more names have five letters than four letters?"

A MY NAME IS: After sharing *A My Name Is Alice* by Jane Bayer (E.P. Dutton, 1992), use interactive writing to create a class book based on the pattern in the book—for example, "G my name is Gavin and my mom's name is Gloria. We come from Galveston and we sell grapes."

TOUCH AND TRACE: Cut out tagboard letters to spell each child's name. Have children glue tactile items such as cotton balls and small pasta shapes on each letter. Let children arrange the letters to spell their name and trace the tactile letters with their fingers.

NAMES PUZZLES: Write each child's name on a sentence strip. Cut each letter apart to make a puzzle. Put each child's puzzle in a recloseable plastic bag. (For practice matching names with faces, glue a photo of each child to the bag and write the child's name on it.) Let children practice putting each other's names together.

BRACELET TRADE: Children pair up to make friendship bracelets to trade with each other. (They can string beads on elastic, or decorate strips of paper that you laminate and fit to children's wrists with Velcro tabs.)

COOKIE CHANT: Write the following chant on a chart:
> *Who stole the cookies from the cookie jar?*
> *[Name of child] stole the cookies from the cookie jar.*
> *Who, me?*
> *Yes, you!*
> *Couldn't be!*
> *Then who stole the cookies from the cookie jar?*

Write each child's name on a sentence strip. Put a piece of Velcro on the chart in the blank where the child's name goes, and on the back of the sentence strips. Place the sentence strips in a cookie jar. Let children take turns using a pointer and reading the chart, and then choosing a name from the cookie jar to put on the chart. Read the chant each time to reinforce children's names.

LINE-UP GUESSING GAME: Line up children one at a time by giving hints about who they are. For example, say "This person has five letters in her name. She has two brothers and a cat." Let children try to guess who you are describing. This helps them get to know each other better.

CHANGE THE NAME: For a fun way to help children learn each other's names, sing "The Muffin Man" but change the name to a student's name and the Muffin Man's address to the address of that child.

JUST-RIGHT READ ALOUDS

Chrysanthemum by Kevin Henkes (Greenwillow, 1991): Chrysanthemum is teased terribly about her name when she goes to school, until a teacher decides to give her daughter the same name. A great book to teach tolerance and differences in kindergarten.

Do You Want to Be My Friend? by Eric Carle (HarperCollins, 1976): This almost wordless picture book about a little mouse who asks many animals to be his friend is great for first-time readers.

Frog and Toad Are Friends by Arnold Lobel (Harper and Row, 1970): This classic tale of friendship and the give-and-take of relationships is always a favorite.

George and Martha Round and Round by James Marshall (Houghton Mifflin, 1988): Five stories about two hippos—George and Martha—and their friendship will spark lively discussions about the subtleties of friendship.

The Missing Piece Meets the Big O by Shel Silverstein (HarperCollins Juvenile Books, 1981): A great book about finding true friends! The wedge-shaped missing piece searches for just the right friend, until he realizes that he has to take some responsibility for a relationship as well.

Wilfrid Gordon McDonald Partridge by Mem Fox (Scott Foreseman, 1989): A little boy befriends the residents of the retirement home next door. This heart-warming tale shows that friends come in all ages!

Weeks 5 and 6: Helping children understand they are valued members of our learning community.

The most important way that we can make each child feel valued as a member of the learning community is by taking a genuine interest in each and every one. It is also important that children know each other well enough to comfortably share their ideas, hopes, and dreams. Using morning meeting to start each day with community-building activities and time to socialize fosters a caring learning community. The following activities extend this sense of community.

Activities for Weeks 5 and 6

EYE GRAPH: In pairs, have children check their eye color. Give each child precut eye-shaped paper representing different eye colors. Have each child add the eye that shows their eye color to a class graph. Math opportunities come out of comparing and contrasting the data on the graph.

HOW HIGH? Measure each child's height. Make a class graph. Repeat this throughout the year to make some interesting comparisons, and to study qualitative change (a student growing taller) as well as quantitative change (how much a student grows in one year).

HANDS AND FEET: Have children partner up to trace each other's full body on butcher paper. Let children use yarn, fabric scraps, and paint to add details, such as hair and facial features. On the hands, help children write what they like to do with their hands, and on their feet, what they like to do with their feet. Give each child a large red paper heart. Help children write a positive comment about their partners on the hearts and glue them to the center of the corresponding tracing.

TISSUE-TUBE PEOPLE: Take a full-body-shot photo of each child. Help children cut out the photo and use clear contact paper to attach it to a bathroom tissue tube. Place these "people" in the block center for children to play with.

Weeks 5 and 6 Sing-Alongs

Continue to learn songs from previous weeks and try some new ones:

"The African Village Song" (from *Dr. Jean Sings Silly Songs* by Dr. Jean Feldman; Crystal Springs Books; 800-321-0401)

"It's a Small World" (from *Disney's Greatest, Volume 2;* Walt Disney Records)

"This Pretty Planet" (from *Family Tree* by Tom Chapin and special guest Judy Collins; Sundance Music)

"Special Me" (from *Dr. Jean and Friends* by Dr. Jean Feldman; Crystal Springs Books; 800-321-0401)

ALL ABOUT ME ON TAPE! Help each child fill in the blanks to an All About Me information sheet. (Use the top of page 197.) If children are unsure of any of the answers, ask their parents. From these information sheets, help children write a narrative about themselves. Attach a picture to the narrative. Compile everyone's narratives into a class book. Read about each child on tape and add both the tape and the book to the listening center.

JUST-RIGHT READ ALOUDS

One way to weave cultural diversity into a unit on friendship is with children's books. Suggestions for books that work well for weeks 5 and 6 follow.

All the Colors of the Earth by Sheila Hamanaka (Mulberry Books, 1999): Children are depicted celebrating the common bond of childhood all over the world.

A Chair for My Mother by Vera B. Williams (Greenwillow, 1982): A child and her mother save their change to buy a chair after their apartment is destroyed in a fire. The community chips in to help out. This is a great story to underscore the concepts of kindness and community.

Horton Hears a Who! by Dr. Seuss (Random House, 1954): Horton will be loyal to those Whos down in Whoville—no matter how small! A book of steadfast friendship!

Like Me and You (Raffi Songs to Read) by Raffi (Crown, 1994): Children mail letters to one another around the world, in the common bond of family.

Loving by Ann Morris (Lothrop, Lee and Shepard, 1990): Photographs of children all over the world accompany a simple but compelling story line.

The Paper Bag Princess by Robert N. Munsch (Annick Press, 1988): Princess Elizabeth teaches Prince Ronald a lesson when she explains that clothes and material things do not make a prince. Kindergartners love this wildly funny tale.

Stellaluna by Janell Cannon (Harcourt, 1993): Stellaluna, a baby bat, is asked to be someone she is not (a very hard thing to do!) when her mother is attacked by an owl and she must live with and act like birds. A great book to foster discussions about being ourselves.

This Is the Way We Go to School: A Book About Children Around the World by Edith Baer (Scott Foresman, 1992): From vaporettos in Italy to helicopters in Alaska, this book celebrates diversity as it depicts the ways children around the world travel to school.

We Are All Alike, We Are All Different by the Cheltenham Elementary School Kindergartners (Scholastic, 2002): Kindergartners will love this book, because it is written by kindergartners!

Throughout the year children will revisit the class book they made, building reading and math skills each time.

Celebrating the Friendship Unit

As the Friendship unit comes to a close, celebrate students' learning with the following activities. In the process, children will revisit skills and concepts they've learned, reinforcing understanding and deepening meaning.

FRIENDSHIP FAIR: Set up friendship stations that children can rotate through—for example, one for making friendship necklaces with a friend, one for sharing a special book about friends, one for making a friendship book, and one for playing a friendship game (such as matching children's names with their photos).

FRIENDSHIP BOOK: Let children partner up with new friends to make friendship mini-books. Photocopy a class set of pages 198–200. (Complete page 6 of the mini-book first, adding a new sentence for children to complete.). Give each child a set of the pages. Have children cut apart the mini-book pages, stack them in order, and staple to bind. Help children work in pairs to complete the books, sharing what they like most about each other and what kinds of activities they enjoy doing together. Bring children together in a circle to share their books about their new friends.

More Kindergarten Themes

- Animals in Winter
- Artists
- Author Studies
- Community
- Creepy Crawly Critters
- Fairy Tales
- Fall Leaves
- Families
- Farm
- Health/Human Body
- Inventions
- Living Things
- Martin Luther King and African-American History
- Native Americans
- Oceans
- Poetry
- Weather

Friendship Book

Make new friends
and keep the old.
One is silver
and the other gold.

By _Kristen_ and _Emilia_   1

FRIENDLY FEAST: Invite parents to school one evening for a potluck dinner. Ask each family to cook a favorite family recipe and bring the dish to share. Compile the family recipes in a classroom cookbook and publish it for all of the families. As part of the evening, let children share with their families some of their favorite friendship activities, books, and projects.

ASSESSING STUDENT LEARNING

During a thematic unit, I often use several different assessments, depending on the children and the activity or project they are involved with. This section offers a look at assessing student learning through observation (both by the teacher and student), rubrics, work folders or portfolios, and culminating activities.

As students record observations over time, look for increased use of detail in their language.

TEACHER OBSERVATIONS: Teacher observations can take many forms. Anecdotal records of observations as children work on activities and projects come in handy for progress reports and conferences. Developmental checklists and curriculum guides are another way to direct and document observations.

CHILD OBSERVATIONS: Child observations involve children observing a place, person, or an item and then drawing and writing about it. These are saved and included as part of the child's thematic folder (or portfolio). I ask children to document their observations when we take a field trip, listen to a guest speaker, or watch a movie. Sometimes children are asked to document observations of their work, such as seeds they have planted, or the activity of insects they're investigating.

RUBRICS: Rubrics of desired behaviors make it easy to document the behaviors children demonstrate during project work. Rubrics should be completed at different points during the thematic unit or project study to provide a record of growth. (For a sample rubric, see page 201.)

Activity Assessment

I write anecdotal records in the margins of my planning pages, which later remind me of activities and strategies that were effective during the unit.

PRODUCTS: Products are anything children produce during the unit of study or project work. These can include their observations, as discussed on page 193. Other products may include any writing they've done as part of the study, art projects, musical pieces (such as songs or dances they may have created that can be audio- or videotaped), or photos of work.

SELF-REFLECTIONS: Self-reflections are opportunities for children to reflect on their own work. Self-reflections help children to see what they've learned over a period of time, and encourage them to navigate their own learning. Self-reflections are great self-esteem boosters, as they are proof of how much a child has grown. (For a sample self-reflection form, see page 202.)

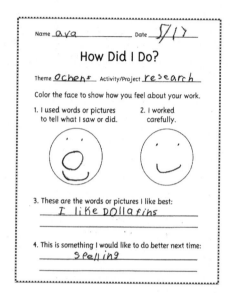

PORTFOLIOS OR THEME FOLDERS: I have each child make a theme or project folder at the end of each thematic unit. The children decorate these folders to match the theme we have studied. They then place all the work they have done for the entire project or theme into the folder. Items in the folder may include products they have made, photos of their work, and self-reflections. Many children come back to me each year and tell me how they still pull out their theme folders to refer to during study in another class, or just to revisit their learning.

CELEBRATIONS OF LEARNING: Celebrations of learning are events that take place at the end of a study unit that allow the children to share what they have learned during that study. These celebrations can include fairs, museums, skits, books the children have made, displays, class-created charts and stories, or interactive writing about a topic. The many ways the children celebrate what they've learned provide opportunities for authentic assessment. Photos, videotapes, audio tapes, and projects can be taken from these celebrations of learning for documentation of student learning.

TEACHER RESOURCES

Emergent Curriculum by Elizabeth Jones and John Nimmo (National Association for the Education of Young Children, 1994): This book follows a child-care center through a year of learning about and using emergent curriculum. Although it is based on a preschool, it offers valuable insight for kindergarten teachers.

Fresh & Fun: Teaching With Kids' Names by Bob Krech (Scholastic, 2000): What's in a name? Find out with dozens of games and activities that build reading, spelling, and math skills, and much more.

Making Themes Work by Anne Davies, Colleen Politano, and Caren Cameron (Peguis Publishers, 1993): This easy-to-read and practical guide describes how to choose a theme and make it work.

The Portfolio and Its Use: A Road Map for Assessment by Sharon MacDonald (Gryphon House, 1997): This book is a very rich resource for using portfolios in kindergarten.

Scaffolding Children's Learning: Vygotsky and Early Childhood Education by Laura E. Berk and Adam Winsler (National Association for the Education of Young Children, 1995): This guide offers clear and concise information about Vygotsky and his impact on the classroom.

Young Investigators: The Project Approach in the Early Years by Judy Harris Helm and Lilian Katz (Teachers College Press, 2001): This book explains how to get started using the project approach.

Thematic Unit
Weekly Planner

THEME _____   DATES _____

WEEK _____

Focus _____

_____

_____

Activities _____

_____

_____

Read Alouds _____   _____

_____   _____

_____   _____

Other _____

_____

_____

Name _____ Date _____

Guess Who!

I like to _____.

My favorite food is _____.

My favorite color is _____.

I have _____ brothers and _____ sisters.

My eyes are _____.

My hair is _____.

My favorite thing to do is _____.

Can you guess who I am?

Lift the flap
to find out!

Friendship Book

Make new friends
and keep the old.
One is silver
and the other gold.

By _____ and _____

My new friend's name is:

_____

I like my new friend because:

_____

_____

_____

_____

3

Our favorite things to do together are:

_____

_____

_____

4

These are some ways my new friend is like me:

_____

_____

_____

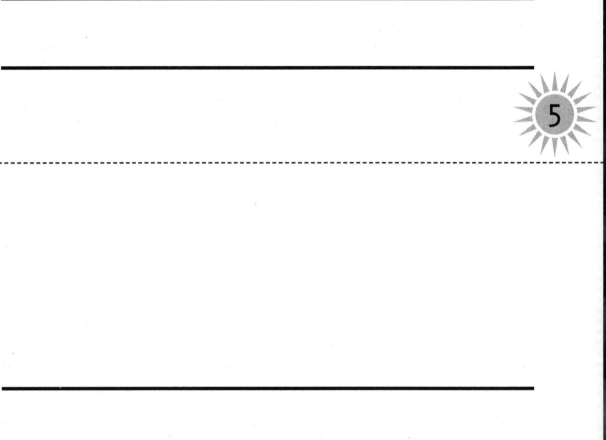

5

- -

_____

_____

_____

6

The New Kindergarten: Teaching Reading, Writing & More • Scholastic Professional Books

Name _____

Date _____

Thematic Unit Rubric

Theme: _____

Project: _____

Behavior	Starting the Project (date)	Investigation Phase (date)	Investigation Phase (date)	Culminating Project (date)
Works well with group members				
Manages time wisely				
Shows self-control				
Stays on the topic				
Asks appropriate questions				
Contributes to the group				
Embarks on project in an organized way				
Accepts ideas of others				
Respects others				
Sees a project through to completion				

Name _____ Date _____

How Did I Do?

Theme _____ Activity/Project _____

Color the face to show how you feel about your work.

1. I used words or pictures to tell what I saw or did.

2. I worked carefully.

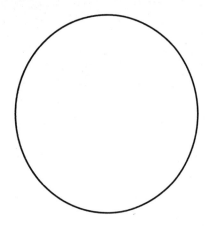 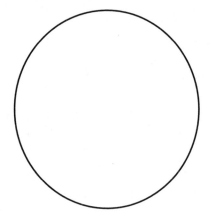

3. These are the words or pictures I like best:

_____

_____

4. This is something I would like to do better next time:

_____

_____

The New Kindergarten: Teaching Reading, Writing & More • Scholastic Professional Books

CHAPTER 1o

Building
Home-School
Connections

Keep in Mind...

"Teachers can't assume that every culture and parent holds the same template for what constitutes an ideal child or a good parent."

—from "Responding to Cultural and Linguistic Differences in the Beliefs and Practices of Families with Young Children" (*Young Children,* May 2000)

Parents are a diverse group; they come to us from many different cultures and family backgrounds. The parents in our classrooms have a vast range of cultural values and models of education, as well as religious and socioeconomic backgrounds. Family configurations are just as varied—from the traditional two-parent family to single parents, families with disabilities, teen parents, grandparents serving as parents, multigenerational families, stepfamilies, blended families, foster families, and same-sex families. Regardless of the differences, parents and families have valuable information about their children.

Parents and teachers ultimately have the same goals for children: we want them to be healthy and happy. We want them to be academically successful and to reach their full potential. We want them to get along with others, make friends, and develop socially. In short, we want to develop self-sufficient, dependable members of our community and of the world. This is a tall order, and is best met when schools and families are mutually supportive of children and of each other. This chapter offers practical advice for making this happen, beginning with making families feel comfortable in the classroom.

WELCOME!

Making parents feel welcome in the classroom is crucial to the parent-teacher relationship and children's success. Effective parent-teacher relationships are built on trust, and parents need to be invited to their children's classrooms for the positive events and activities that help to build that trust. Sharing in the day-to-day activities in the classroom is a non-threatening way for parents to become involved in their children's education. When teachers establish an open-door policy with parents and stand by it, parents become more comfortable with the teacher and the classroom. Open-door classrooms allow parents to see that teachers are compassionate and competent.

In my classroom, I try to open the doors to parents before the school year starts. I want to tap into the resources that the families have to offer our classroom, and to build relationships with families that will support children in our classroom. Following are strategies and activities for building this home-school relationship, beginning before the school year starts and continuing all the way to June.

Before the School Year Starts

FAMILY SHARING: One way we can make children and their families feel more comfortable in our classrooms is by honoring families and their cultural differences. Inviting families to share with the classroom and teacher some of their family routines and celebrations is one way to do this—for example, ask them to share some of their favorite songs and stories. Reading and singing these songs with the class in days to come reinforces the connection between the child's home and school.

GETTING TO KNOW YOU: In the spring of the year before the new kindergarten starts, our school holds an open school night for parents of incoming kindergartners. This gives parents a chance to look around the kindergarten classrooms, meet with the teachers, and get an overview of the program. During this same week, the children are invited into the kindergarten classrooms to visit. These events help to answer questions that parents might have about kindergarten, and help them to be more comfortable with the transition.

GOALS AND EXPECTATIONS: Different parents have different goals and expectations for their children. These goals and expectations are reflected in the communities, societies, and cultures from which they come. For example, most American traditions, based on Western societies, put an emphasis on independence and self-reliance, whereas many Asian and Latin American societies focus on cooperation and collaboration. Obedience and conformity are important to other immigrant groups, such as the Vietnamese. Parenting roles and expectations also differ from culture to culture. Talking with families about your own beliefs, values, and experiences and asking them to share their perspectives helps build strong teacher-family relationships.

KINDERGARTEN AMBASSADORS: When incoming kindergartners and their families come for a visit, I have current kindergartners serve as "Kindergarten Ambassadors" and show the visitors around the classroom. During the visit, we read a book that our current class has made about kindergarten. Our visitors take a tour of the school, and finish up with a stop in the cafeteria for a snack.

Just a Reminder

It's important at this time to remind parents that they are viewing the classroom in the spring, when children are almost first graders and are comfortable with the routine. Let parents know that when their children begin school, the classroom will look much different.

Kindergarten Screening

Our school used to conduct screening tests for incoming kindergartners during the spring, but we recently decided to change the screening date until children have comfortably settled into school in the fall, usually October. Screenings are completed as part of our regular classroom routine. We usually find a quiet place, like the library, and screen children one-on-one during the school day.

SUMMER ICEBREAKERS: A few weeks before the start of school, I call or visit each family. I want the family to know me as a person, and feel comfortable coming to me with questions and concerns throughout the school year. This is a good time to talk with families about their perceptions of school and kindergarten, and to discuss goals for their child. In this conversation I also share my goals and philosophy of teaching. However, the main objective of this first parent visit is to help break the ice and open the lines of communication.

PRESCHOOL VISITS: After the open school night in the spring, I visit each of the preschools that children will be coming from. I like to see how they interact in the school setting. I also want them to meet me on a more personal level and to know that I care about them. Most of the children get very excited to meet their new kindergarten teacher at preschool. It's also a good time to check with the preschool teachers to find out if there is anything I can do to make the transition more comfortable for incoming students and their families.

Meeting children before the start of kindergarten helps ease their anxiety.

TRANSITION WORKSHOP: Our community's local family center sponsors a workshop for parents in the spring called "Transitioning Your Child into Kindergarten." This workshop has been helpful for many parents who are unsure of what kindergarten is like today. Parents usually have questions about how much sleep a typical kindergartner needs, what kind of schedule works best to prepare children for kindergarten, and what to do to ease the anxieties of their children. These workshops are most helpful if a number of kindergarten teachers from the district are able to attend and help answer questions.

KINDERGARTEN PICNIC: About a week before school starts, our school hosts a kindergarten picnic. Families of incoming kindergartners are invited, as well as the school's kindergarten staff. Each family brings dinner and we enjoy getting to know each other and seeing the kindergarten classrooms. I try to have a picnic project that each family can work on ahead of time, so that we have a tangible memento of the start of our school journey. Some years the families make a quilt, other years I've had them make a large puzzle, with each family decorating a piece to represent something special about their family. (See page 21.) I give each family a packet to take home that details everything they will need to know about kindergarten, from lunchtime routines to the daily schedule. I also request that parents write to me about how they see their child as a learner and as a person. (See reproducible send-home, pages 213–214.)

August 30, 2001
Welcome to Kindergarten!
  We are excited to start a fun-filled year of learning and growing together!
  Please take a minute to make a family quilt square. The supplies are found on the back art table.
  Also, check the attached dismissal list to make sure we have the proper dismissal procedure for your child. See Mrs. L. if there are changes.
  Have fun!   Mrs. L. & Mrs. D.

This message welcomes families and invites them to work on a class project.

The First Few Weeks of School

FIRST VISITS: Within the first few days of school, I call each household. Many parents are very anxious about the transition to kindergarten, and this call helps to address any questions or concerns they have. The key to communicating with parents is to start early, before they begin to worry too much over things that might be minor and easily explained. I want this first contact of the school year to be very encouraging, and keep the information shared as positive as possible.

FAMILY SNACK: After children have settled into the classroom routine, I start having parent volunteers come in to help out, including setting up the Family Snack. Families take turns bringing a snack to share with the class (about one day per month). I encourage parents

Inventory Parents In

Parent visitors and volunteers will appreciate getting a quick overview of the day. Other tips to keep in mind:

Parent visitors and volunteers will appreciate getting a quick overview of the day. Other tips to keep in mind:

- Let parents know (if needed) that classroom time is not a time for in-depth conversations, but offer to set up a time to meet outside of class time if necessary.
- Be sure parents who are helping know classroom procedures in advance. For example, how much help do you want children to get with answering questions?
- Make parents aware of any classroom rules. For example, how do children ask for help? Do they raise their hand, or approach the teacher or helper?
- Set a positive example for parents.

Parents appreciate a list of ideas for healthy snacks. Sliced fruit is always a favorite.

to spend time in the classroom when they bring in the snack, helping to set up the table or assisting in some other way.

VOLUNTEER CHECKLIST: I like to welcome families right away, and let them know that they are encouraged to spend time in the classroom. One way to do this is with a volunteer checklist, which lets parents choose from a list of ways they can help out. I keep the list very broad so that every parent can find some way to be part of our classroom. (See sample checklist, page 215.)

PARENTS' NIGHT: About six weeks into the school year, we host a fall kindergarten parents' night. With the new emphasis on academic standards, parents want to know what their children will be learning, and what our methods for teaching it are. This is a good time to explain how you integrate your philosophies with the curriculum objectives. For example, if you hold a developmental philosophy, explain how children will be challenged academically while learning in a play-based kindergarten. Share the rich opportunities for writing and literacy learning during Choice Time, as well as games that reinforce number and math concepts. I like to have the district curriculum guides on hand for parents to peruse. This lets them know that I am aware of the kindergarten objectives determined by our district, and lets them know what those objectives are. Parents often like to know what they can do to help their children at home, and this is a good time to suggest ways they can participate.

As the Year Continues

DAILY NEWS: At the end of each day, just before dismissal, the children and I discuss what we did during the day. This is a good time to remind children of all of the wonderful activities and projects they've done. The daily news serves as a memory jogger, so when children get home from school and their parents ask, "What did you do in school today?" they don't say, "Nothing!" After we write the daily news, I like to sing a song with the children so that they leave the classroom happy and upbeat. Seeing their children coming home from school happy communicates volumes to parents.

April 25, 2002

We planted SEEDS in our aquarium. We planted radishes lettuce, onions, carrots, and Beet We watered our seeds. We made a graph of what we thought would GRow. Most people thought lettuce would grow fastest.

Dismissal is a great time to practice a little public relations. I use the daily news to remind students of all of the wonderful activities we did during the day. When children leave, they are excited to share their good news with their families.

FRIDAY FOLDER: I write each child's name on a simple two-pocket folder at the beginning of the year. This serves as the "Friday Folder." Children take it home each Friday with all of their work and information from the week. Parents know when this will come home, and it gives them the weekend to look over their child's work at leisure. When it comes back on Monday, I put a sticker on the back. Children love to collect stickers, and it gives them an incentive to return the folder.

WEEKLY REVIEW: Include this form (page 216) in the Friday Folder to highlight information about a child's activities and successes for the week and goals for the next. Help children complete the first five sections of the form. Add comments you would like to share with families before sending it home. Families can respond to the comments, and then add their own, sign at the bottom, and return the paper to school. These weekly reviews provide regular documen-

Keep in Mind...

Some parents are unable to read. Other parents can't read English. It is important to find alternative ways of communicating with them, such as with telephone calls, audiotapes, and translated copies of material.

Send-Home Page

Parents like to be able to extend their child's learning at home. For a send-home page packed with activities that make the home-school connection, see page 217.

tation of children's work and progress during the year. It's helpful to revisit them periodically to notice how children's goals change throughout the year, as well as how their writing skills improve.

WEEKLY NEWSLETTER: The most basic form of communication to parents from the classroom is a newsletter. Newsletters range from fancy to informal. Computer technology today can help enormously with designing newsletters, and even allows you to include digital photos. My newsletter goes home every Friday in the Friday Folder, so that parents know when to expect it. I use a template for the newsletter so that parents know what to look for: what happened during the week, what the plans are for the following week, and reminders. Upcoming events are included under "On the Horizon." It's always good to keep in mind that newsletters do not have to relate every event of the week. They're an overview and can serve as a springboard for discussions at home. (For a reproducible newsletter template, see page 218.)

News From Kindergarten Winter Wonderland

This Week: January 7-11, 2002
This week was spent researching animals in winter and making large models of the animals. The children also made snowflakes to enhance our display of animals in winter. The children worked in groups on these animals and each group has written a "report" about their animals. We also studied the letter "W" for winter this week. In Letterland "W" is called "Wicked Water Witch". We have been reading many stories about winter and animals in winter. We have learned some new songs about winter this week as well. It was nice that the weather cooperated this week and sent us some snow for our winter unit!

Next Week: January 14-18, 2002
We will begin studying the letter "T" or "Ticking Tom" as we learn more about trees and the animals that live in them in winter. The children will be making a tasty winter treat for the birds using pine cones covered with peanut butter and bird seed. Later in the week they will make Jack Frost windows-depicting what Jack Frost does to our windows in winter time. Throughout the week the children will continue to work in small "book clubs" and read to and with the teachers as usual!

Reminders:
Each time your child is the helper of the day they will be coming home with a cloth bag that contains a book and activities for you to do with your child. Please enjoy this with your child and return it promptly on the next school day. Each child will get a turn with each homework book/activity bag before we switch to a new activity. This takes the place of the M&M Homework for now. Thanks!

January 18-January book order due.
January 25-January Homework due.
January 21-Martin Luther King Jr. Day-No School
Thanks for all the interest in chaperoning our field trip to Polly Hill Arboretum!

"I've learned that the best classroom in the world is at the feet of an elderly person." -Andy Rooney

Share an inspirational message with families as part of your weekly newsletter.

PRESS RELEASES: Beyond sending home a weekly newsletter, I like to send press releases to the local paper about events happening in our classroom. Children love to find articles about their classroom in the newspaper. They're powerful tools for helping the community to understand both how their tax dollars are being spent and the important work teachers are doing with their youngest citizens.

PARENT-TEACHER CONFERENCES: Scheduled parent-teacher conferences are a time-honored tradition in America's schools. This is the time when parents get to hear how their child is performing in the classroom. Parent-teacher conferences are an important means of communication, and we can make them even more effective and family friendly. We all know how hard it can be to say everything in the 15 or 20 minutes alloted for each conference. If at all possible, stagger conferences to avoid feeling rushed. Small touches at conferences can also make a big difference: To make sure everyone's comfortable, for instance, be sure to provide adult-size chairs for parents. I send a letter home before the first conference, asking parents what two or three goals they have for their child. We discuss these goals during the conference, and then refer back to them during the year to note progress. Parents' goals for their children are often the same as mine, which gives us a common bond right from the start. This also lets me know how I can support families throughout the year, modifying and selecting strategies and programs that will help meet their goals.

PARENT WORKSHOPS: Parents are usually very grateful when they are invited to a workshop that has been planned with their family in mind. For example, Literacy Night invites parents to an evening of games and activities they can do at home with their children. Math Night gives everyone a chance to make some games and activities to take home. You may or may not choose to include children in these workshops. If not, arranging for child care at the school is appreciated by many parents.

HOME-SCHOOL NOTEBOOKS: Home-school notebooks are an effective means of two-way communication between teachers and parents. Home-school notebooks allow parents to voice concerns and share successes, and let teachers address any questions parents might have. Children with special needs often carry a notebook from home to school so parents and teachers can share essential information about the child's program and/or medical issues. Many special needs children have hidden talents and skills that are only demonstrated in the comfort of their own home; this knowledge is very helpful to teachers. Children who are nonverbal benefit tremendously from the use of a home-school notebook; it is the link between parents and teacher. I use the notebooks for different children at dif-

Conference Reminders

In addition to meeting parents at the classroom door and giving them a warm and friendly greeting, keep these tips in mind for successful conferences:

- Give parents total attention while they are speaking.
- Let your body language convey that you are listening and that parents are respected.
- Restate parental concerns and recognize their feelings.
- Focus on one issue at a time.
- Let parents know that you are not placing blame.
- Respect family circumstances.
- Accentuate the positive.
- Show compassion.
- Let parents know times you are available to follow up with them about information you've discussed.

Including Everyone In Special Events

When planning events for parents to attend, keep in mind parental constraints. Try to offer a variety of times. For example, one activity may be a morning activity, another may be during the afternoon or evening. Be cognizant of child care and transportation needs. Try to include everyone and consider all family situations, offering events for "special guests," not just Mom or Dad.

ferent times. (The idea of writing in thirty home-school notebooks each day is overwhelming.) Sometimes I'll send home a notebook with a child who is ready to take the jump into literacy and is becoming a reader; other times I use it for a child who has me perplexed and about whom I'd like more information.

HOMEWORK: One way in which I support parents in my classroom is through "homework." Homework for young children is not developmentally appropriate and should never be considered mandatory. The homework in my classroom is really a smorgasbord of activities that parents can do with children, including literacy-building book bags (see page 110), interactive mini-books (see pages 170–174), and an optional monthly homework paper with several activities to choose from. I want to support family time with the homework, not disrupt it. The more time families spend talking and interacting with their children, the more literate the children will be.

CELEBRATIONS OF LEARNING: Throughout the school year, celebrations of learning invite parents in to see what children have been learning. Children might put on a play, or act as curators at a "museum" in which their work is featured. These are special times in the classroom and children are always proud to show off their work.

A celebration of the "marriage" of *q* and *u* culminates our fairy tale unit.

Dear _____,

In anticipation of the new school year, I would like to welcome you to our classroom. I'm looking forward to getting to know your child and working with you to make this a wonderful kindergarten year. Our classroom is sensitive to the strengths and needs of each child. Because you are the person who knows your child best, I would like to invite you to share thoughts about your child that you think might be helpful for me to know. Your reflections will help me to better match my teaching style and the curriculum to your child and his or her individual needs.

1. What do you enjoy most about your child?

   _____

   _____

2. What sorts of things is your child most interested in learning?

   _____

   _____

3. What are some of your child's favorite books or things to read about?

   _____

   _____

4. Does your child enjoy being read to? If so, is there a favorite time to read?

   _____

   _____

5. If your child watches TV, what are some favorite programs?

   _____

   _____

6. What games does your child like to play?

_____

_____

7. When your child is upset, what are some strategies that you find helpful?

_____

_____

8. When your child has conflicts with other children, what are some ways he or she works them out?

_____

_____

9. Does your child nap? If so, for about how long?

_____

_____

10. About how many hours does your child sleep at night?

_____

_____

Is there anything else you'd like to share about your child?

Thank you!

Name _____ Date _____

Volunteer Checklist

Dear Families,

Young children love their families to be connected to their classroom, and this connection makes transitions from home to school much easier. We sincerely invite you to be part of our classroom community! Here are some of the ways you might help out. Please check any that interest you. Complete the form and return it to school with your child. Thank you!

Sincerely,

_____

_____ Share family traditions or a special skill.

_____ Pick up and return books at our local library.

_____ Recycle the juice cans/bottles we use at snack time.

_____ Help count and collect the lunch money.

_____ Help with literacy activities in the classroom.

_____ Type stories at home.

_____ Make books on tapes for children.

_____ Cut things out and prepare projects in advance at home.

_____ Help cover bulletin boards and create displays of children's work.

_____ Help out on field trips.

_____ Share information about community resources.

_____ Lead or help out with a craft or cooking project in the classroom.

_____ Bind classroom books at home.

_____ Help set up for a new thematic unit of study.

Please let me know the best days/times to reach you: _____

Telephone number: _____

E-mail address: _____

Name _____ Date _____

Weekly Review

Here are some things I did this week:

1. _____
2. _____

Here are some things I learned this week:

1. _____
2. _____

A book I read this week is:

Title: _____
Author: _____
Illustrator: _____

I am most proud of my work on: _____
because _____

Next week I plan to work on: _____

Teacher Comments: _____

Family Comments: _____

Parent/Guardian Signature _____

The New Kindergarten: Teaching Reading, Writing & More • Scholastic Professional Books

Learning at Home

Dear Families,

Learning never stops! Children love to continue learning at home. The following activities are all fun and easy to incorporate into your daily routines. They'll provide your child with opportunities to make connections between what we're learning at school and the real world. Some of the skills these activities address include sight-word vocabulary, alphabet recognition, phonics, counting, estimating, number recognition, measuring, and patterning.

Sincerely,

Math Activities

✿ With a standard deck of playing cards, ask your child to order the numbers from least to greatest and greatest to least. Or let your child make sets of numbers and sets of colors.

✿ Hide two or three coins in a sock. Don't let your child see! Ask your child to identify the coin by feeling the shape and size. (This helps with estimating measurement and discriminating between sizes.)

✿ On paper, trace the outline of some kitchen utensils and other small household objects. Ask your child to find the objects that fit the outlines. (This uses investigation skills and builds reasoning skills.)

✿ Give your child a bowl of dried beans, grapes, or any small object. Ask your child to estimate how many will fit in his or her hand, then take a handful and count. Discuss how close the estimate was.

✿ Observe the moon. Each night, cut a paper plate to look like the shape of the moon and date it. Save each plate, and let your child put them in order by date. Does your child notice any patterns?

Literacy Activities

✿ Set a group of items on the table (for example, a plate, a spoon, and a cup) and ask your child how they are related. Variation: Add one item that is not related and ask which item does not belong and why. (This encourages thinking and speaking skills.)

✿ Using a small, standard puzzle that comes on outlined cardboard, write an uppercase letter on the back of each puzzle piece. On the corresponding shape on the board, write the lowercase letter to match the uppercase letter. Ask your child to put the puzzle together.

✿ Give your child your "junk mail." Let your child use a highlighter to find all the Gs in the junk mail (or any other letter, as you see fit).

✿ Turn off the TV and make a "No TV Survival Kit." Include favorite books, games, and puzzles. Add a bag of popcorn and camp out in the living room!

Kindergarten News

Week of _____

@ This Week @

@) Next Week (@

@ On the Horizon @

The New Kindergarten: Teaching Reading, Writing & More • Scholastic Professional Books

CHAPTER 11

Ending the Year

Throughout the school year, the classroom becomes a family of learners supporting each other, learning, and growing. As the year draws to a close, we're happy for the break, yet sad to say goodbye. June always brings a sense of accomplishment to me as I look back over the year's learning experiences. As educators, we are truly blessed to work with children and see proof of our joint accomplishments with them and their parents. Very few occupations offer such rewards.

Just as it is important to build a community of learners and a classroom atmosphere that is conducive to learning, it is important for children to bring closure to their year. Doing so allows them to share that sense of accomplishment for themselves, and gives them tangible evidence of their effort and growth that they can take with them as they move forward. Here's how to make the last few weeks just as meaningful as those before.

Meet the Teacher

When the year is beginning to wrap up, I have children meet their next year's teachers. I try to make sure that they have at least one or two friends with them. This is just a short visit, about thirty minutes, but it gives children a chance to ask some questions and see their new classroom. When children come back from this experience, they are usually excited about first grade. During the last few weeks of school, I try to take a moment to introduce parents to their child's new teachers as well.

Easing First-Grade Fears

Some children will feel anxious about embarking on a new grade. I like to remind them about some worries they may have had about kindergarten, and how successful they've been. Discussing fears can also help ease the transition. Depending on the school, some of the differences between kindergarten and first grade that may make a child anxious include:

- Amount of choice time.
- Number of new classmates.
- The use of desks instead of tables.
- The expectation to read.
- Consequences for inappropriate behavior.
- The use of the "big" bathroom in the hall (not in the classroom).
- Length of school day.
- Elimination of rest time.
- The use of lined paper.

Anxiety Easer

Some children need extra support when making transitions. In such cases, I try to ask the child's new first-grade teacher to visit our classroom from time to time, even if just for a brief "hello." As the child begins to see the teacher on a regular basis, and sees that I am friendly with this teacher, anxieties diminish. The child and I also visit the new classroom a few times before the end of the school year.

Make a List, Check It Daily

During this time of year, even children who are usually on task have a hard time concentrating. Our schedules often get disrupted for special events and field trips in the warm weather. Children who normally have a hard time attending or negotiating social situations may struggle. To tone down this excitement and calm children's nerves, I plot out the remainder of the year, making a list that shows children what work we still need to get done. We check the list daily, which helps children see their accomplishments and set new goals.

Rule Reminders

Toward the end of the year, children usually need a solid reminder of the class rules. I often engage children in a discussion about what makes the classroom work, and how we can continue our important work through the end of the school year. Sometimes children will say that they need more breaks, so we might have more recesses (which are shorter in length). Of course, they always like to say that extra treats will help them, too, and I do try to make the end of the year a little more special by surprising them with some extra fun activities sprinkled throughout the last few weeks of school.

Send-Home Survey

I like to send home a survey to parents asking how I can improve home-school communication. I also send a survey about the newsletter to learn what parents found helpful. Overall, it's important to leave the school year feeling good about relationships with families, because they share their experiences with other families who you may someday find in your classroom.

Passing the Torch

About a month before the end of the year, our class makes a book for incoming kindergartners, complete with photos. This book gets children thinking about what they've learned over the year and all they have accomplished. The veteran kindergartners are very proud of their achievements, and love to tell the incoming students all about kindergarten.

A class-made book about kindergarten lets incoming students and their families get acquainted with the program.

Children share the book with the incoming kindergartners when they visit the classroom in late May or early June. At this visit, I pair current kindergarten children with incoming children and they spend some time getting to know each other. They'll check in with each other in September, which gives each child something to look forward to. Many new first graders remember how much they appreciated this when they were in kindergarten and make a point to stop by to say hello to their new friend and see how kindergarten is going.

SARAH october 2001

Sarah is happy and interested in school. We can always count on Sarah to know exactly what is going on in class!

Children's writing on each monthly addition to their keepsake books serves as a wonderful record of how much their writing skills grow in one year!

TiP

Planning Celebrations

I try to schedule large-scale classroom celebrations well before the school year ends. I like to save the last two weeks or so to bring closure to our year in a more calm way. It's comforting to have time with children so we can enjoy each other and not be pressured to perform late in the school year.

Keepsake Books

At the end of the year we have a celebration to honor a special person in our lives. At this celebration we present our special guests with books that we've been making all year. Children complete a page in their books each month, including the month, year, and their signature. Each page of a child's book features a project of some sort and something special about that child. Every other month we measure their height and record that on the corresponding page. The books are beautiful and serve as a very complete reminder of a child's kindergarten year. Families love them!

Celebrating Summer Birthdays

Many teachers have a class party at the end of the year to celebrate summer birthdays. In my classroom, I assign each child who has a summer birthday a pretend birthday near the end of the school year. On this child's pretend birthday, we celebrate their birthday just as we would any other birthday during the school year. This means that the child's family is invited to bring in the snack on the pretend birthday, and the child is the helper of the day and gets all of the other perks associated with a birthday.

More Kindergarten Keepsakes

Other projects that serve as kindergarten keepsakes include:
- Recipe books with all the recipes they have made throughout the year.
- Song books with favorite sing-alongs.
- Good-bye books that include photos of classmates and space for signatures and notes.
- Time lines with dated photos of children working and learning together.
- Archives of the daily news reports that we have recorded throughout the year; this serves as a written history of our kindergarten year.

Leave the Room Looking Great

We've built our community of learners all year, and children are proud of their classroom. As part of giving the year a good send-off, they leave the room looking great for the next class. This helps them appreciate how they have come full circle. One of the ways children help prepare the classroom for the next year is by choosing how to cover bulletin boards. They think back to what was important to them when they first walked into the classroom, and help select colors and papers. Students leave a "legacy" on one bulletin board for incoming students. This legacy is presented with a picture, so it is easily understood by the incoming kindergartners.

One child's legacy for the incoming kindergartners: "I leave all my favorite songs that we sang in kindergarten."

Summer Fun

For six-year-olds, summer seems like a long time! Near the end of the year, I send home several handouts for families, including fun summer activities families can enjoy together, information about summer reading programs at local libraries, and so on. These activities help to bridge the gap for children over the long summer. I also like to send home articles to parents—regarding TV viewing, for example, and ways to limit it—to help facilitate smooth transitions for young children.

Fade Free

Lightly tack newspaper over completed bulletin boards to keep them from fading over the summer.

A Picnic With Parents

We are fortunate to have a park very close to our school, so on the last day of school I invite the parents for a picnic in the park. We all bring bag lunches to keep the picnic low key. This gives everyone time to say their goodbyes, and it gives me time to touch base informally with parents. We all walk back to the classroom, gather our things, and go home. The year ends as it began, with a picnic for families.

Here are some easy how-tos for a few kindergarten staples.

Homemade Blocks

If you do not have blocks in your classroom, try making some. Ask a builder or lumberyard to save wood scraps for you. Cut the wood into blocks, making several of each size. Sand the wood to prevent slivers. Also, ask children to bring in boxes of all sizes. Fill them with newspaper and tape the openings to make building blocks. Be creative—a thick birch tree branch cut into chunks and sanded makes very appealing cylindrical blocks.

Make a Magic Quiet Stick

Use old soda bottles and fill them with glitter, food coloring, and water, or a mixture of Caro Syrup, food coloring, and glitter. Be creative. Remember to hot-glue the top on (teacher only). Children can use these magical wands during morning meeting when they need to relax.

Flubber

In a metal bowl mix:
- 1½ cups warm water
- 2 cups white "school" glue
- food coloring

In a clear bowl mix and dissolve:
- 4 t. borax
- 1⅓ cups warm water

Add the glue mixture to the borax solution. Do NOT mix or stir. Wait a few hours and the consistency will begin to solidify. It is ready when very little, or no, liquid is left.

Perfect Play Clay

- 3 cups water
- 3 cups flour
- 3 T. baby oil
  (You can use vegetable oil, but baby oil smells better!)
- 3 T. cream of tartar
- 1½ cups salt
- food coloring (optional)

Mix first five ingredients in a large saucepan. Stir constantly over medium heat until mixed well, about 15 minutes. When cool, knead in food coloring. Store in a covered plastic container or recloseable bag.

Skin-Color Paint Proportions

A great way to make skin-color paint: mix red, white, and black paint. Adjust the proportions to create the desired skin tone.